ABC LETTER TRACING COLORING BOOK & PUZZLE WORKSHEETS FOR KIDS AGES 2-4 & 4-8

My Best Alphabet Toddler Coloring Activity Book With Letters, Shapes, Puzzles & Cute Animals

By

Thrive Creative Kids

© Copyright 2020
Thrive Creative Kids | All Rights Reserved.

No part of this book or the material in it may be cited from or replicated in any way by means such as printing, scanning, photocopying, or otherwise without the prior written authorization of **Thrive Creative Kids.**

**HAVE A QUESTION OR FEEDBACK?
LET US KNOW!**

EMAIL: info@thrivecoloringbooks.com

WEBSITE: ThriveColoringBooks.com

THIS BOOK BELONGS TO:
_____
_____
_____

Aa Apple

A _____

_____

a _____

_____

Trace Letter A

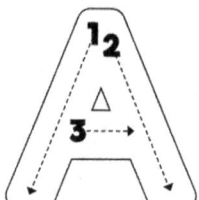 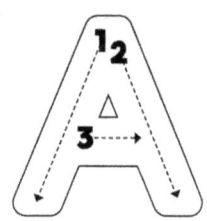 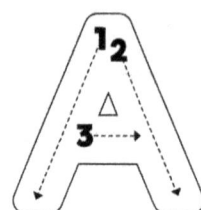 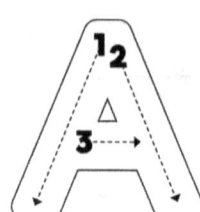 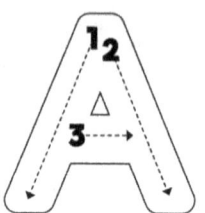

Practice Letter A

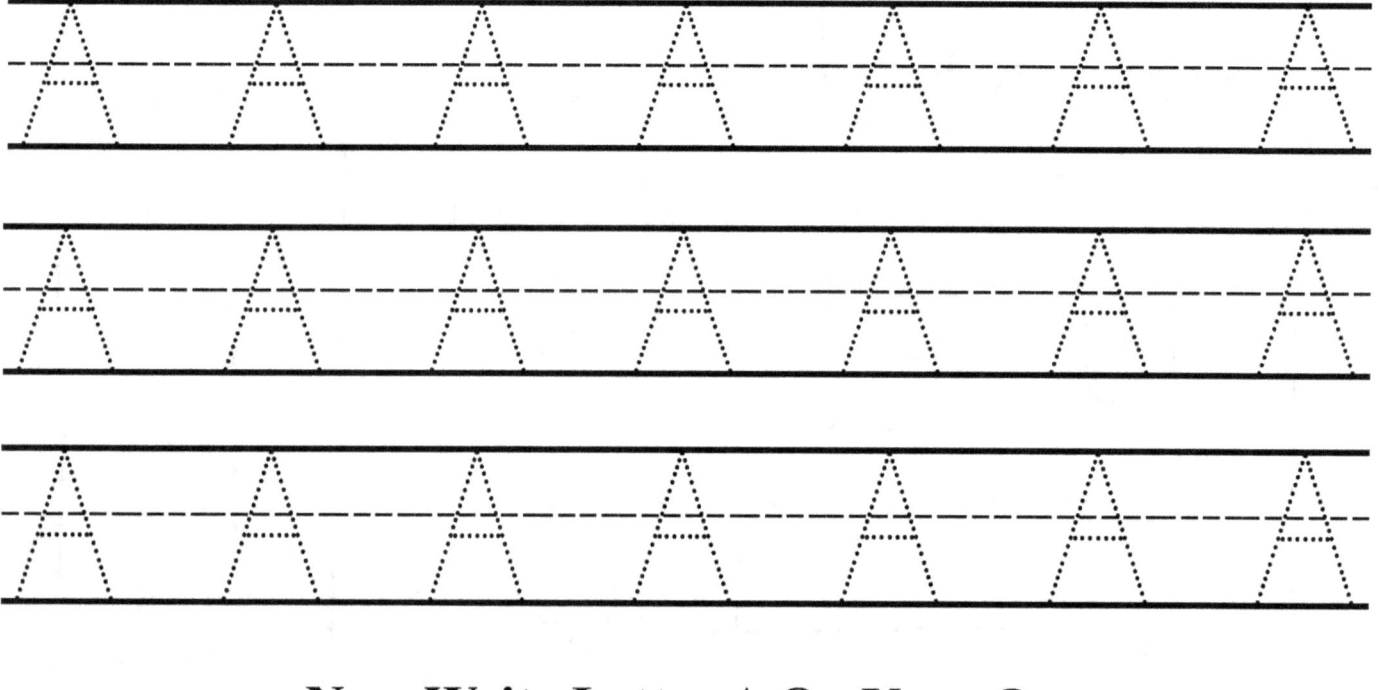

Now Write Letter A On Your Own

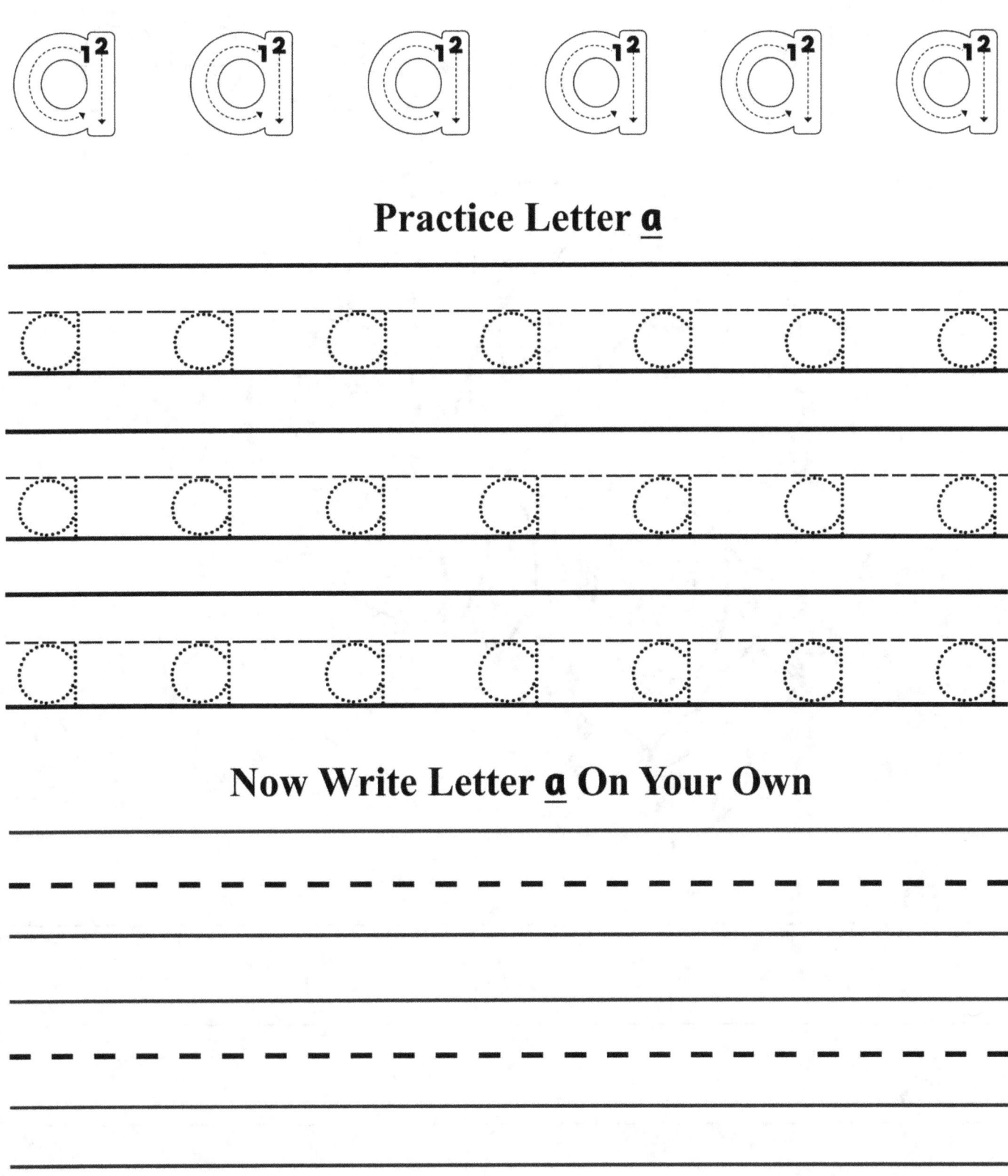

Bb   Bee

B _____

_____

b _____

_____

Trace Letter B

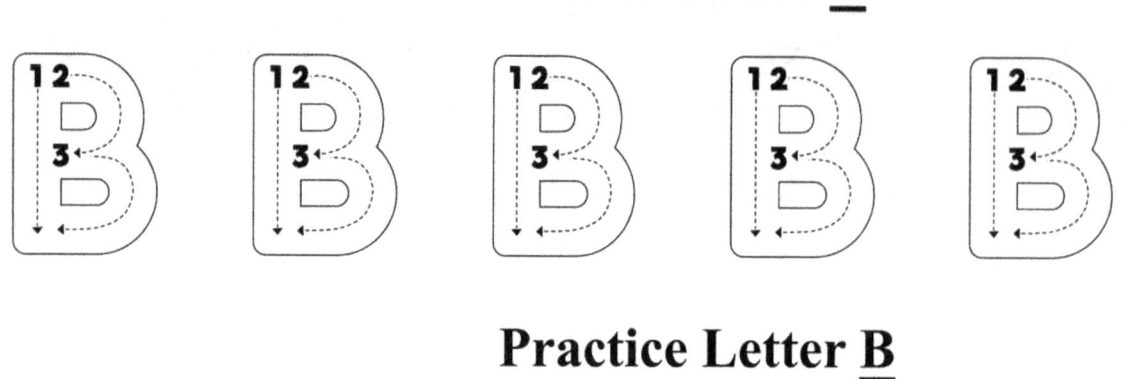

Practice Letter B

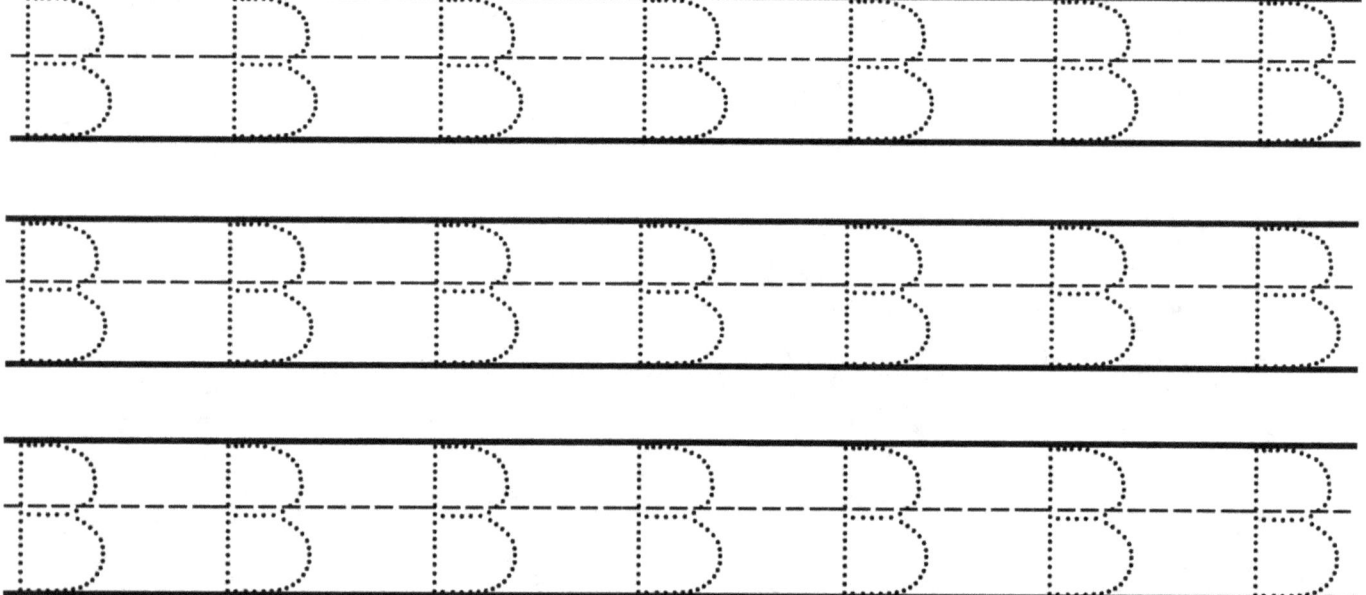

Now Write Letter B On Your Own

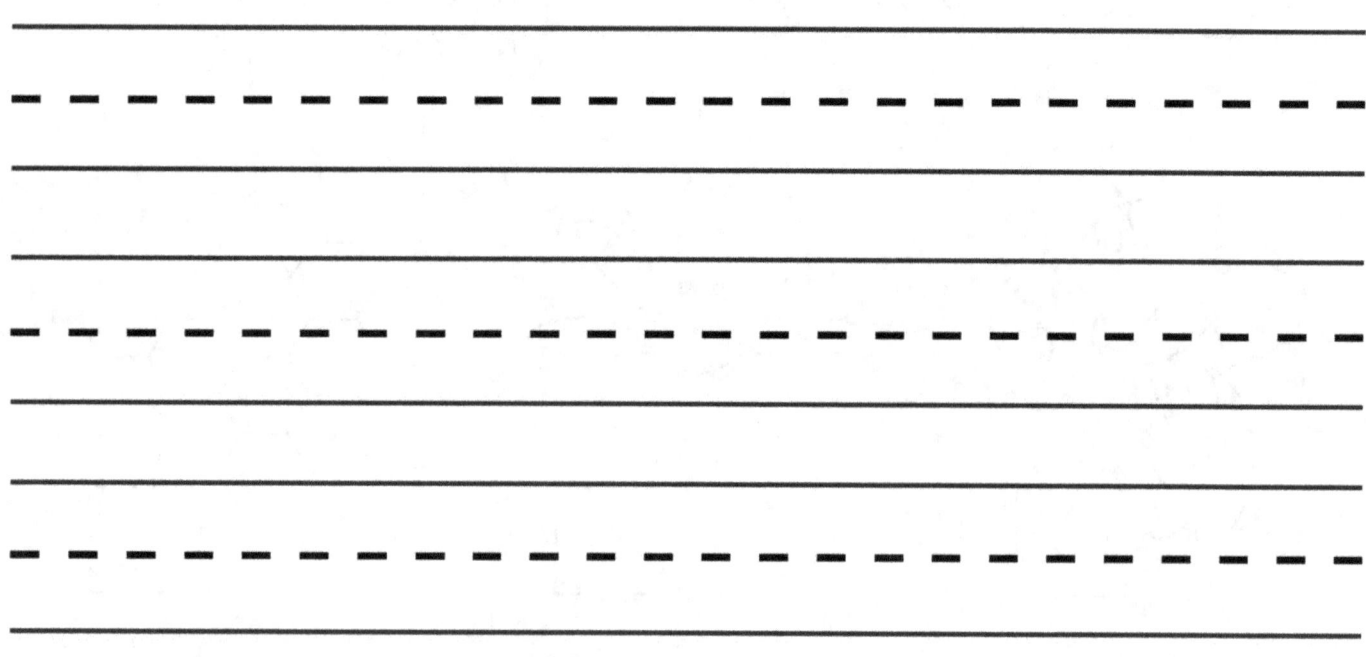

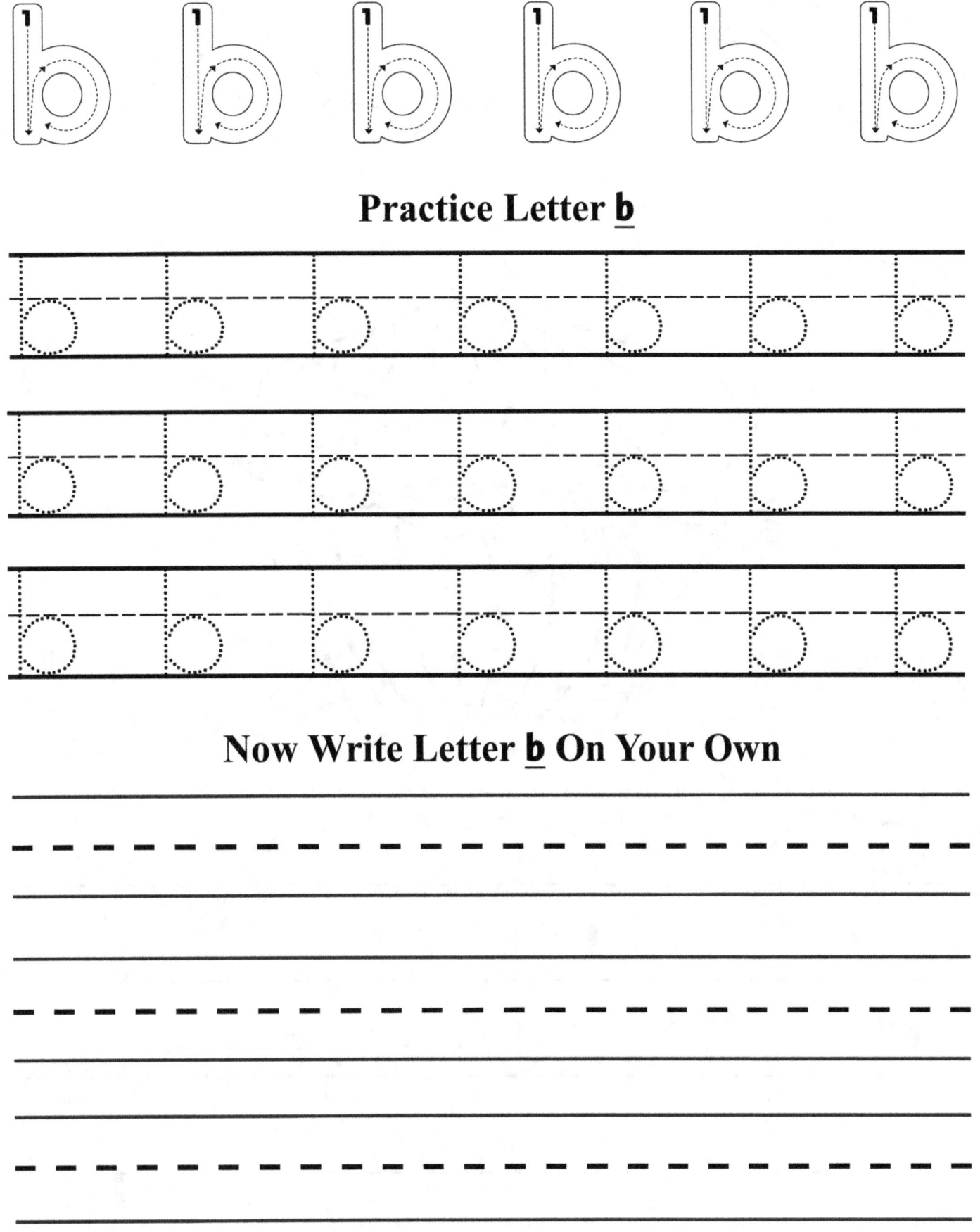

Cc   Cake

C
_____

_____

c
_____

_____

Trace Letter C

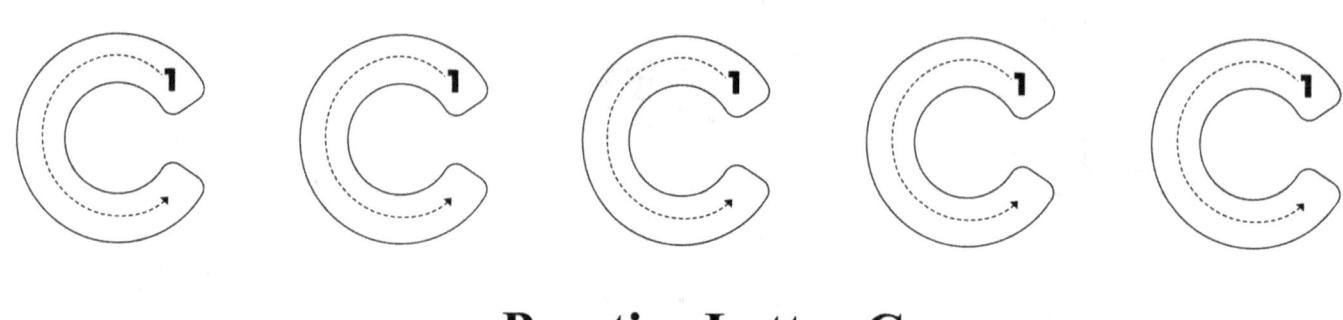

Practice Letter C

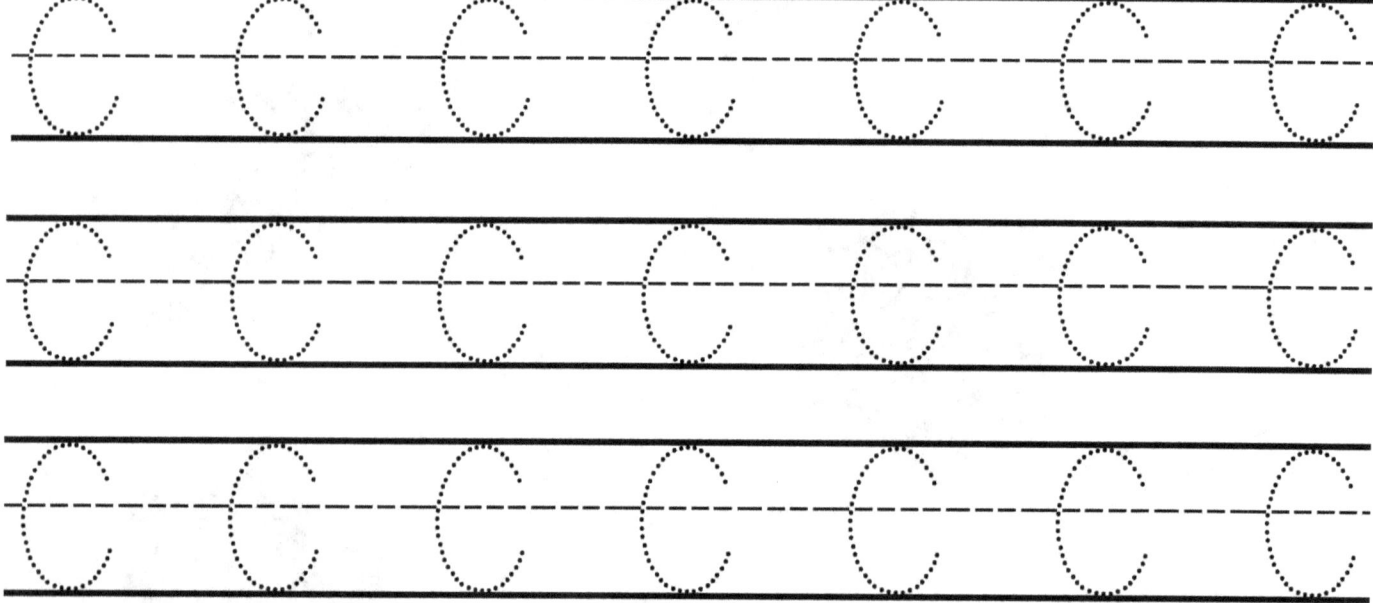

Now Write Letter C On Your Own

Trace Letter c

Practice Letter c

Now Write Letter c On Your Own

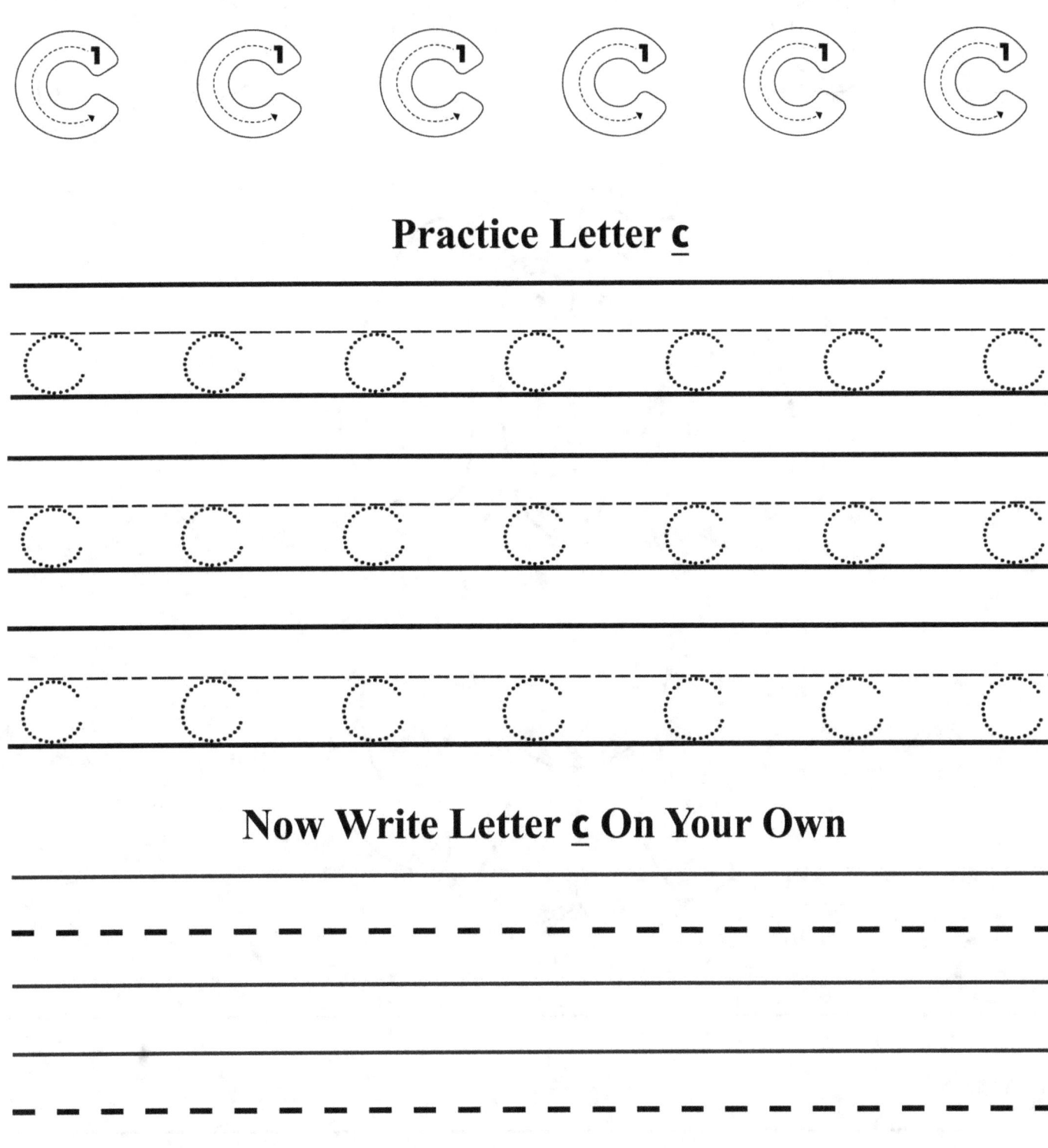

Dd   Dog

D _____

d _____

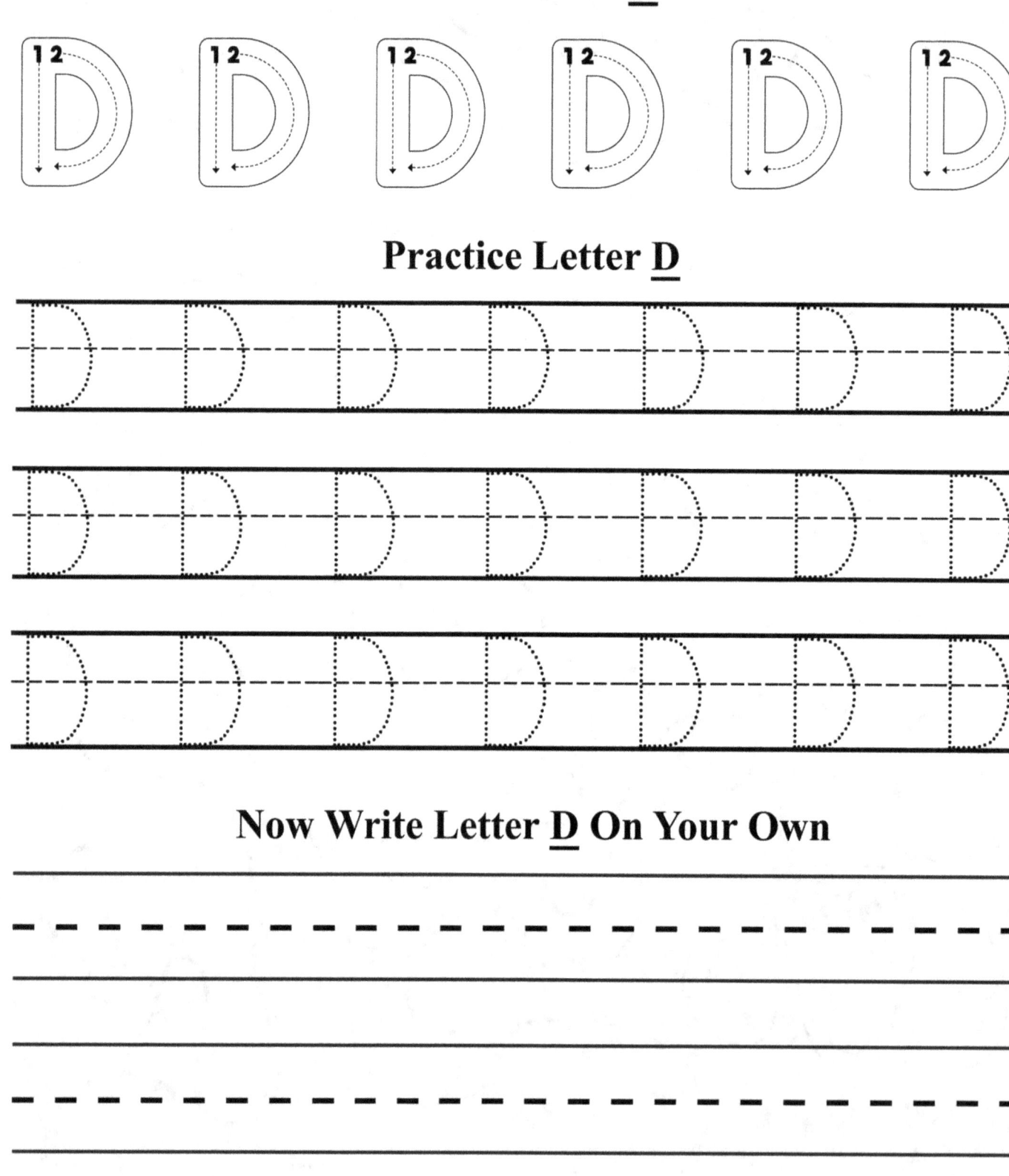

Trace Letter d

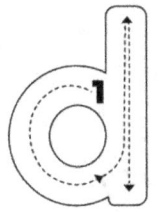 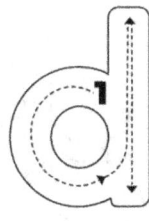 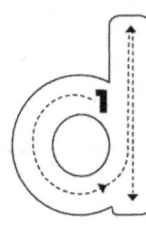 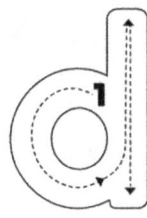 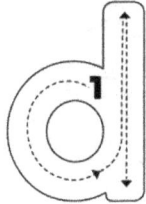 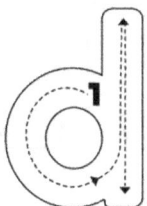

Practice Letter d

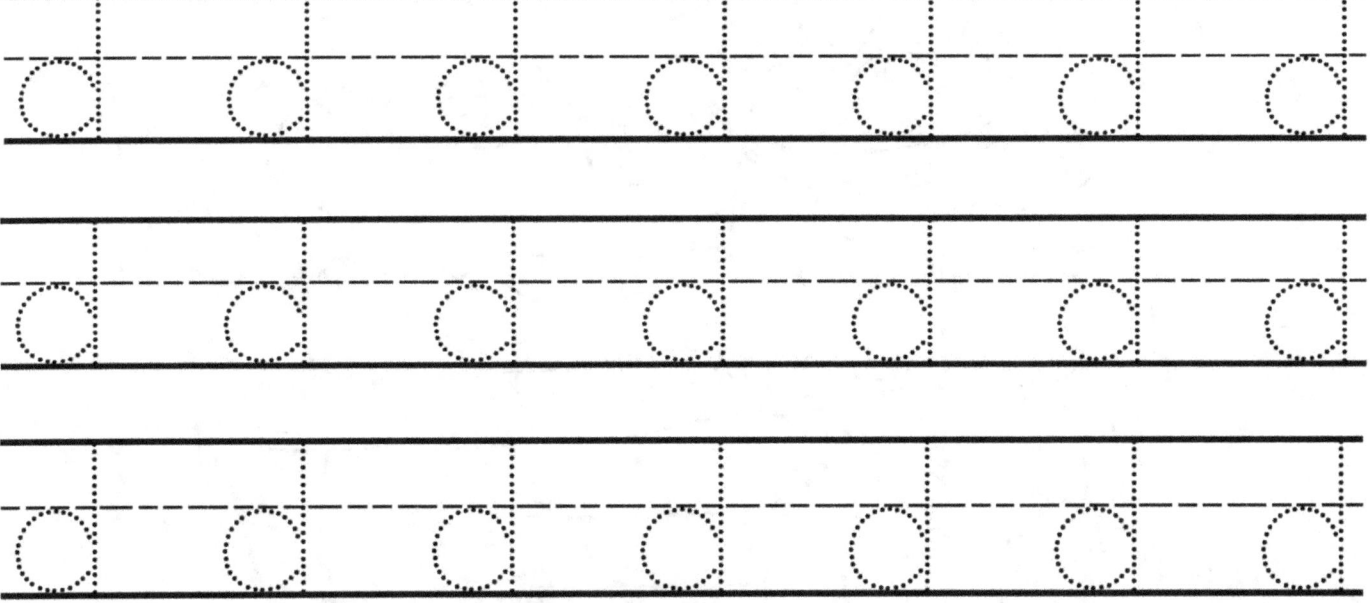

Now Write Letter d On Your Own

Ee   Egg

E _____

_____

e _____

_____

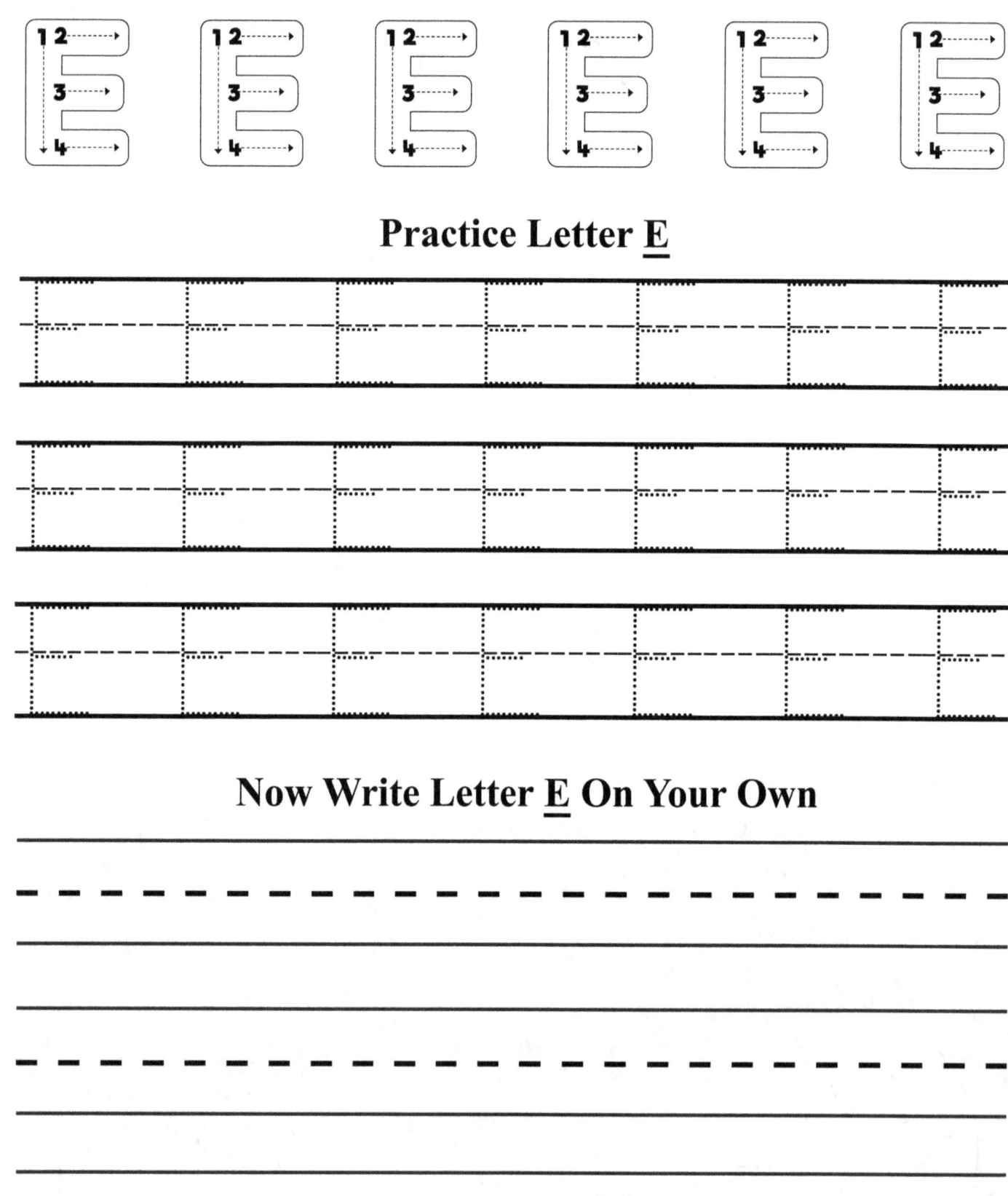

Trace Letter e

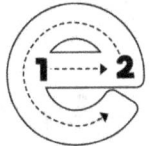 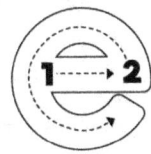 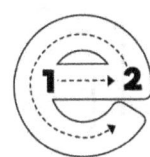 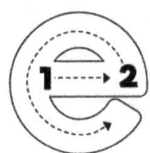 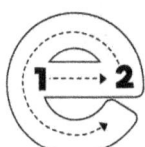 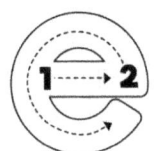

Practice Letter e

Now Write Letter e On Your Own

Ff   Frog

F _____

f _____

Trace Letter F

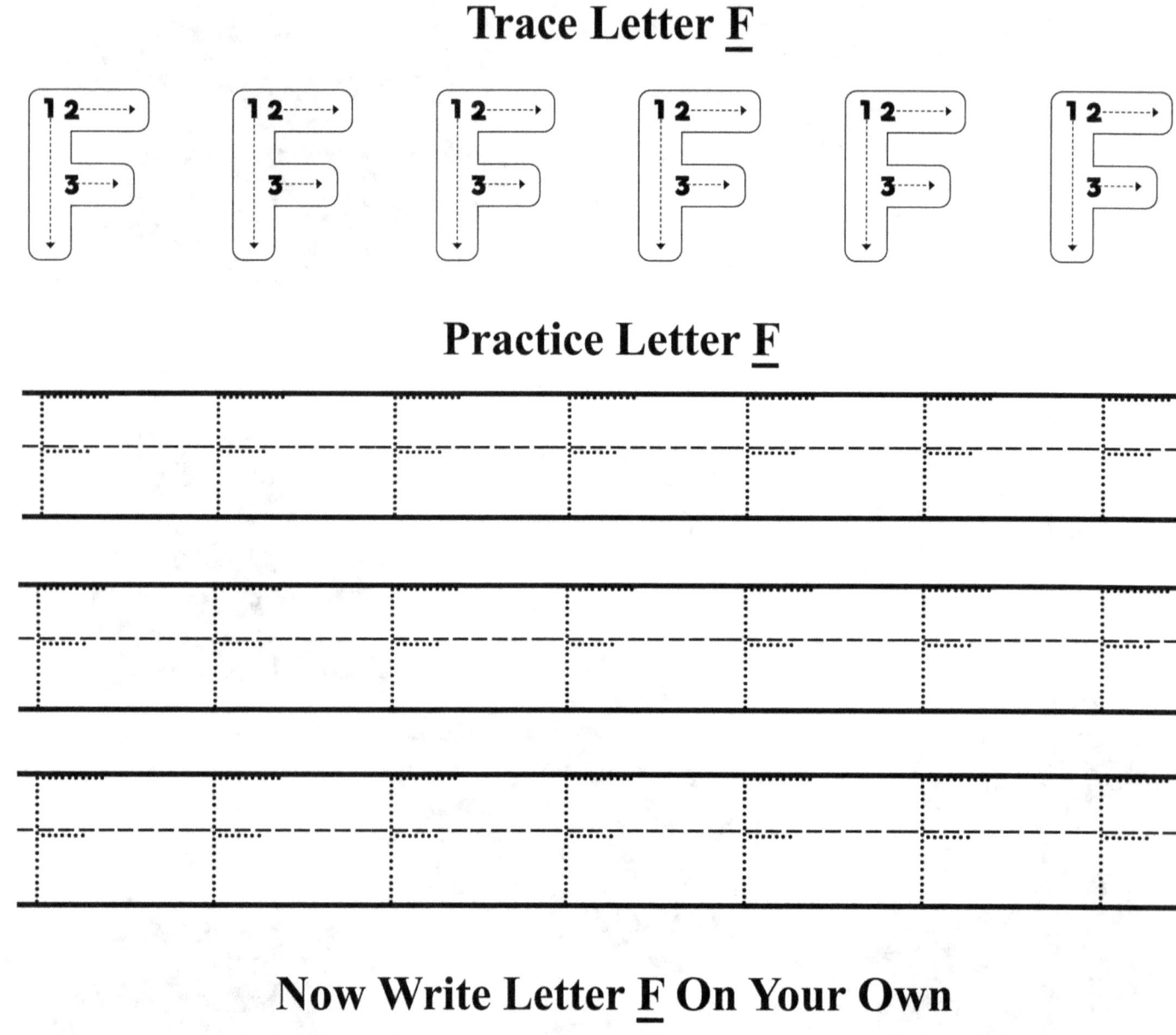

Practice Letter F

Now Write Letter F On Your Own

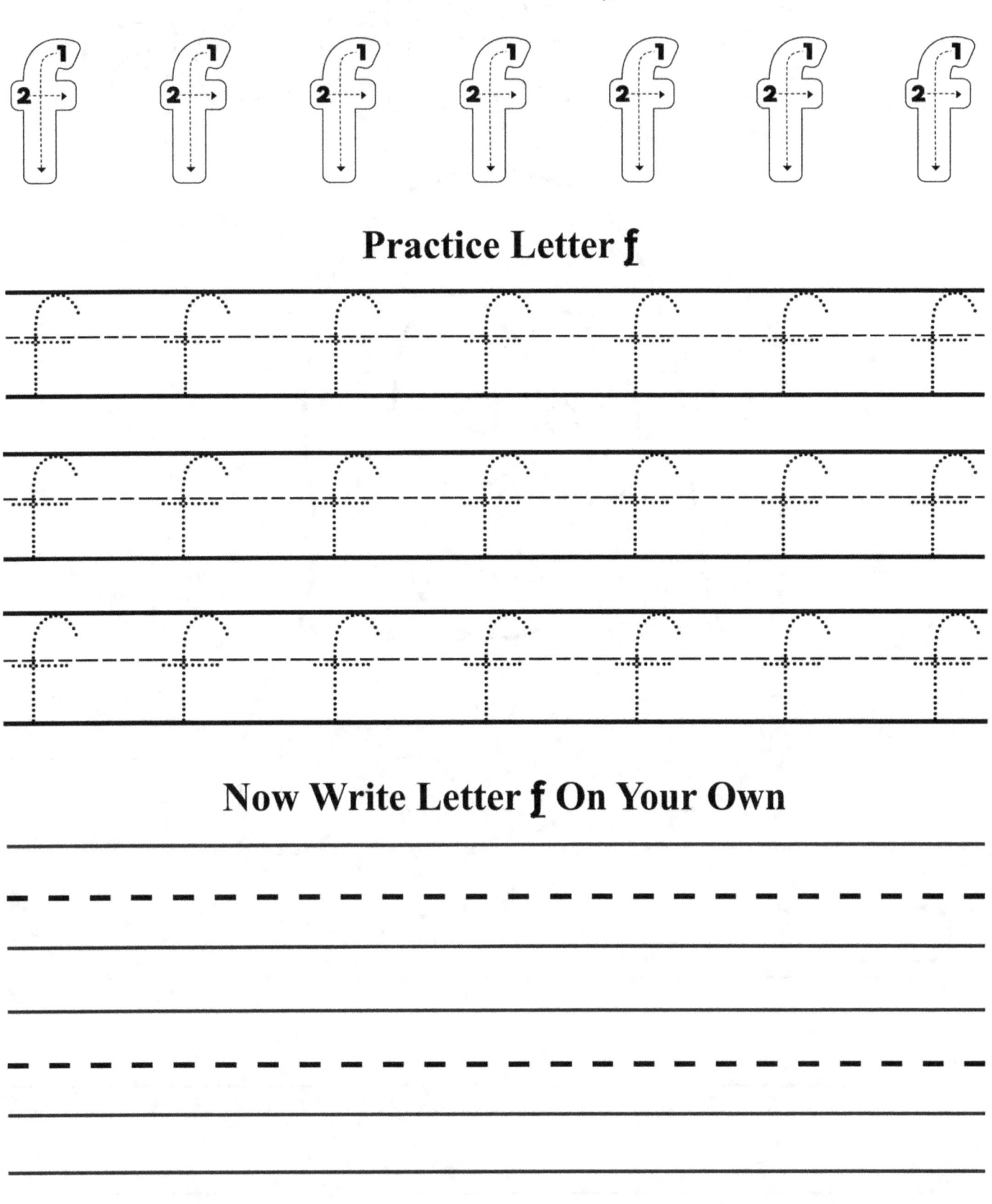

Gg Ghost

G _____

_____

g _____

_____

Trace Letter G

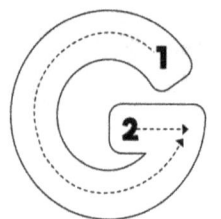 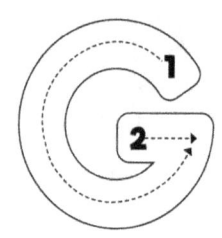 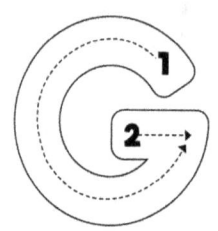 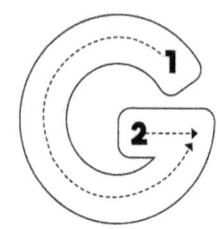 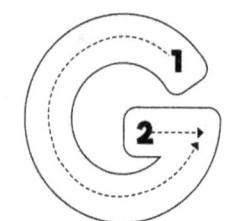

Practice Letter G

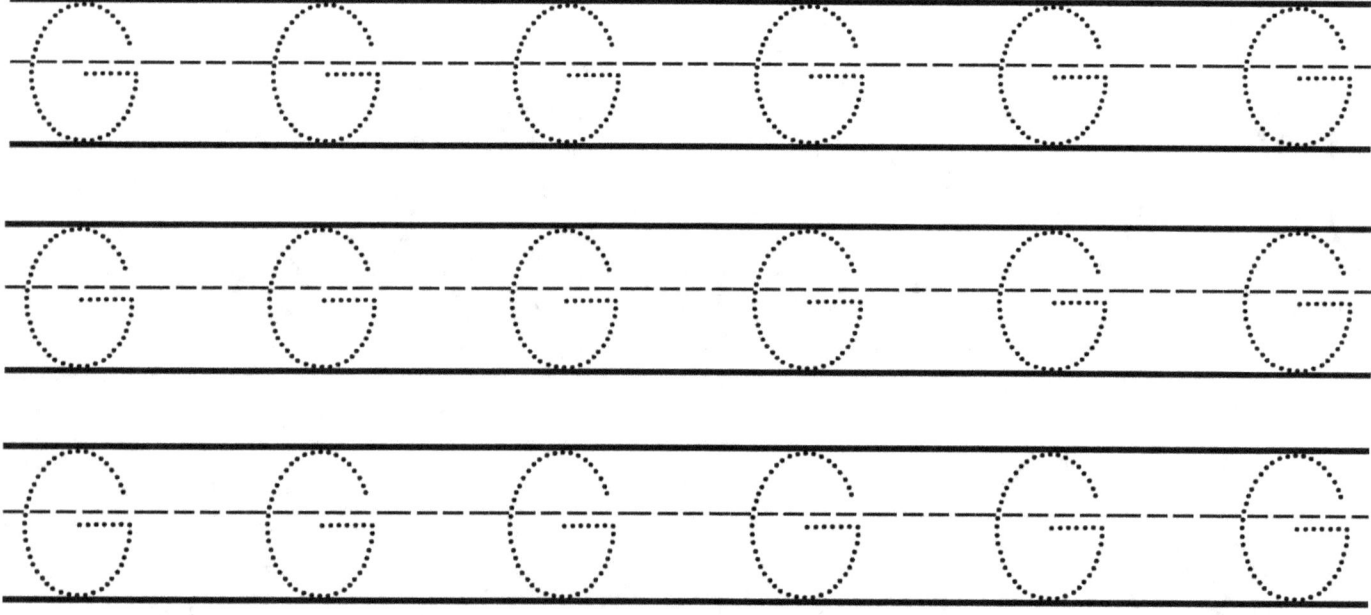

Now Write Letter G On Your Own

Hh   Hare

H _____

h _____

Trace Letter H

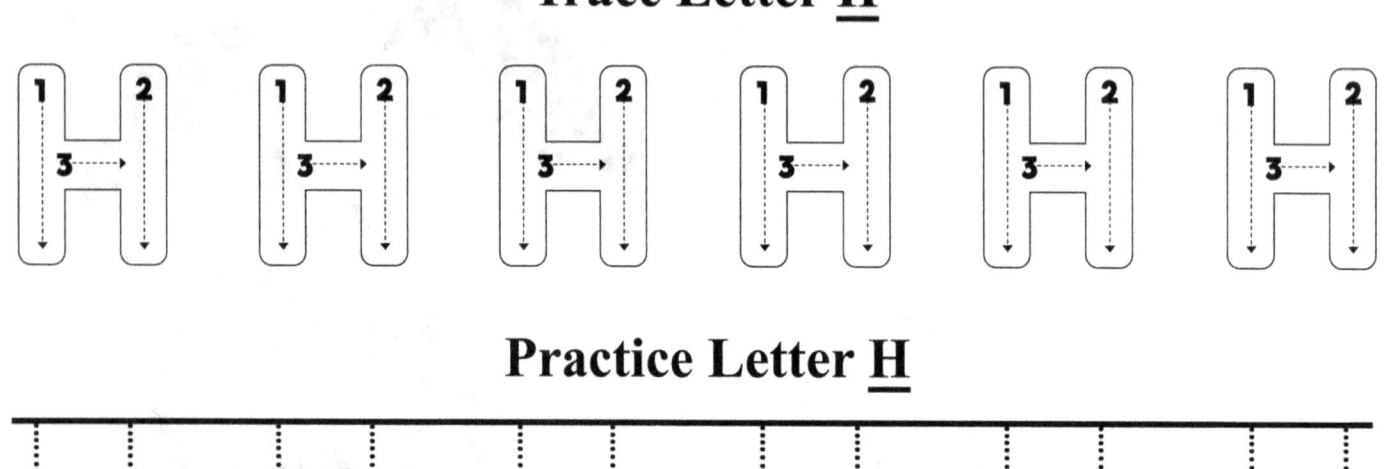

Practice Letter H

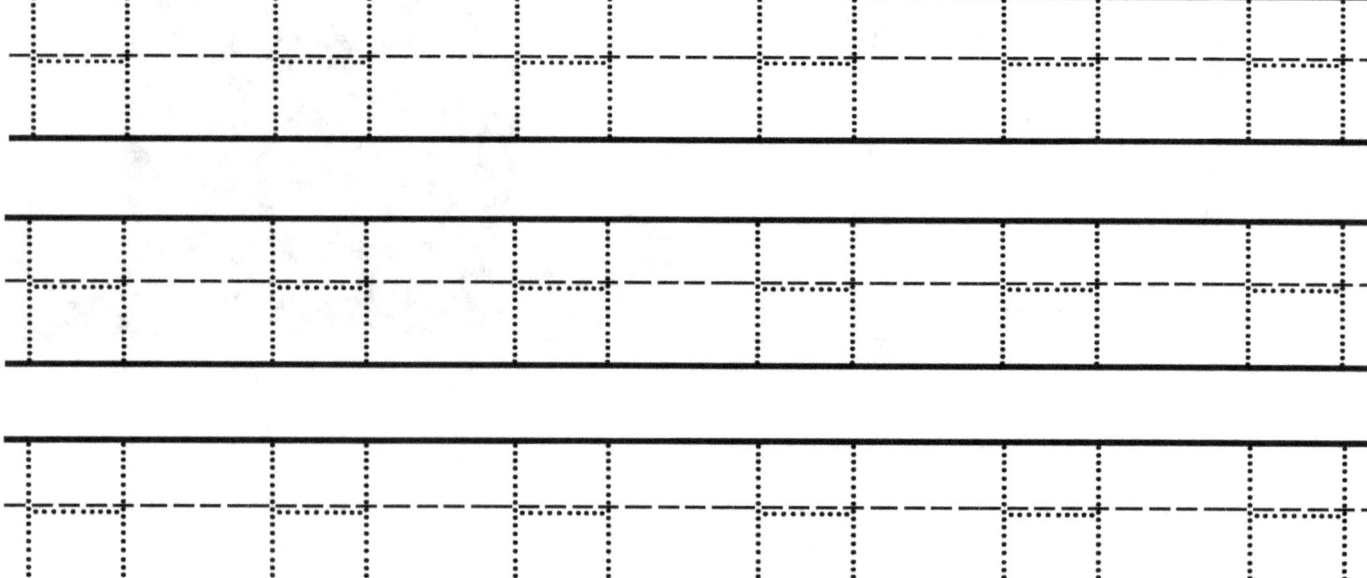

Now Write Letter H On Your Own

Trace Letter h

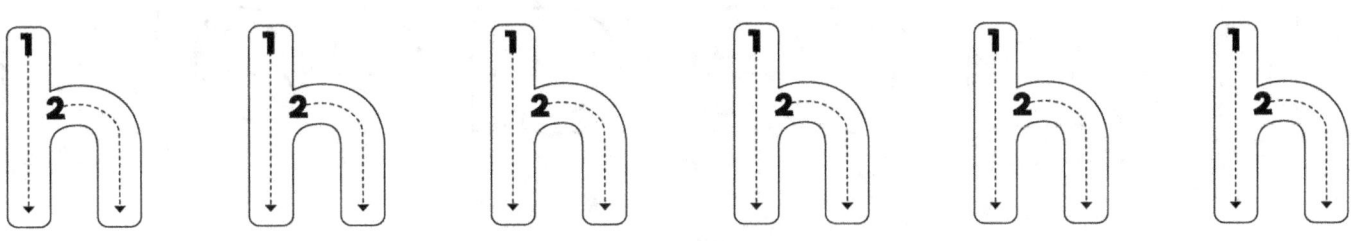

Practice Letter h

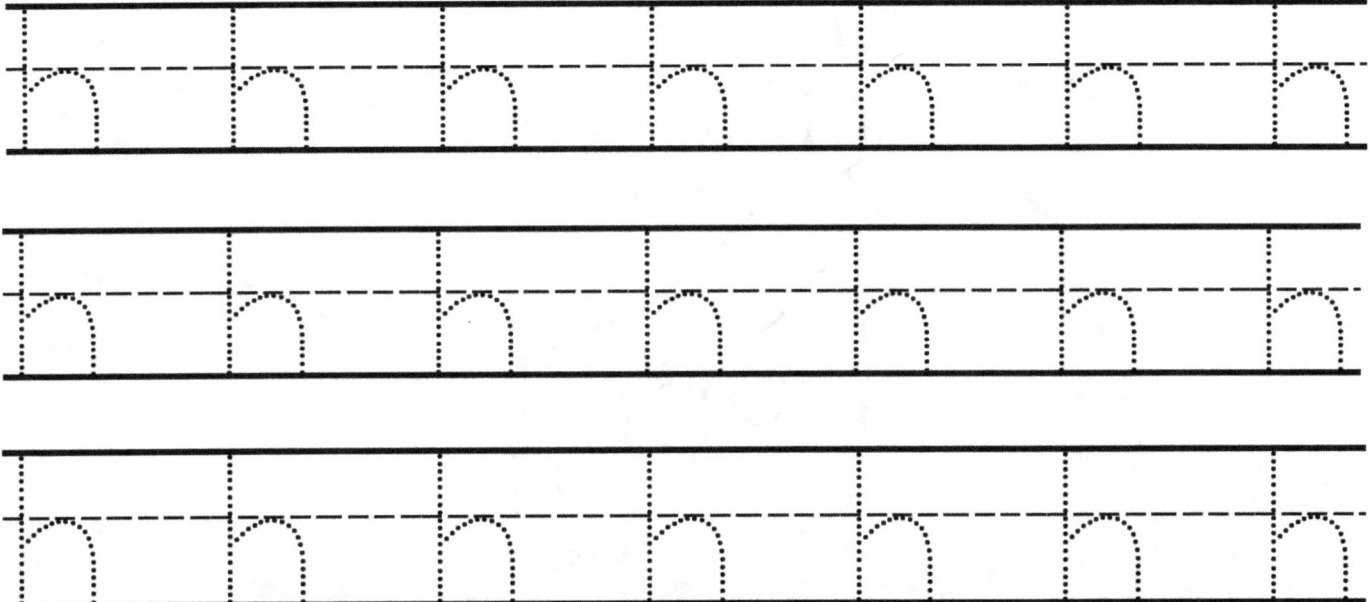

Now Write Letter h On Your Own

Ii Ice cream

I

i

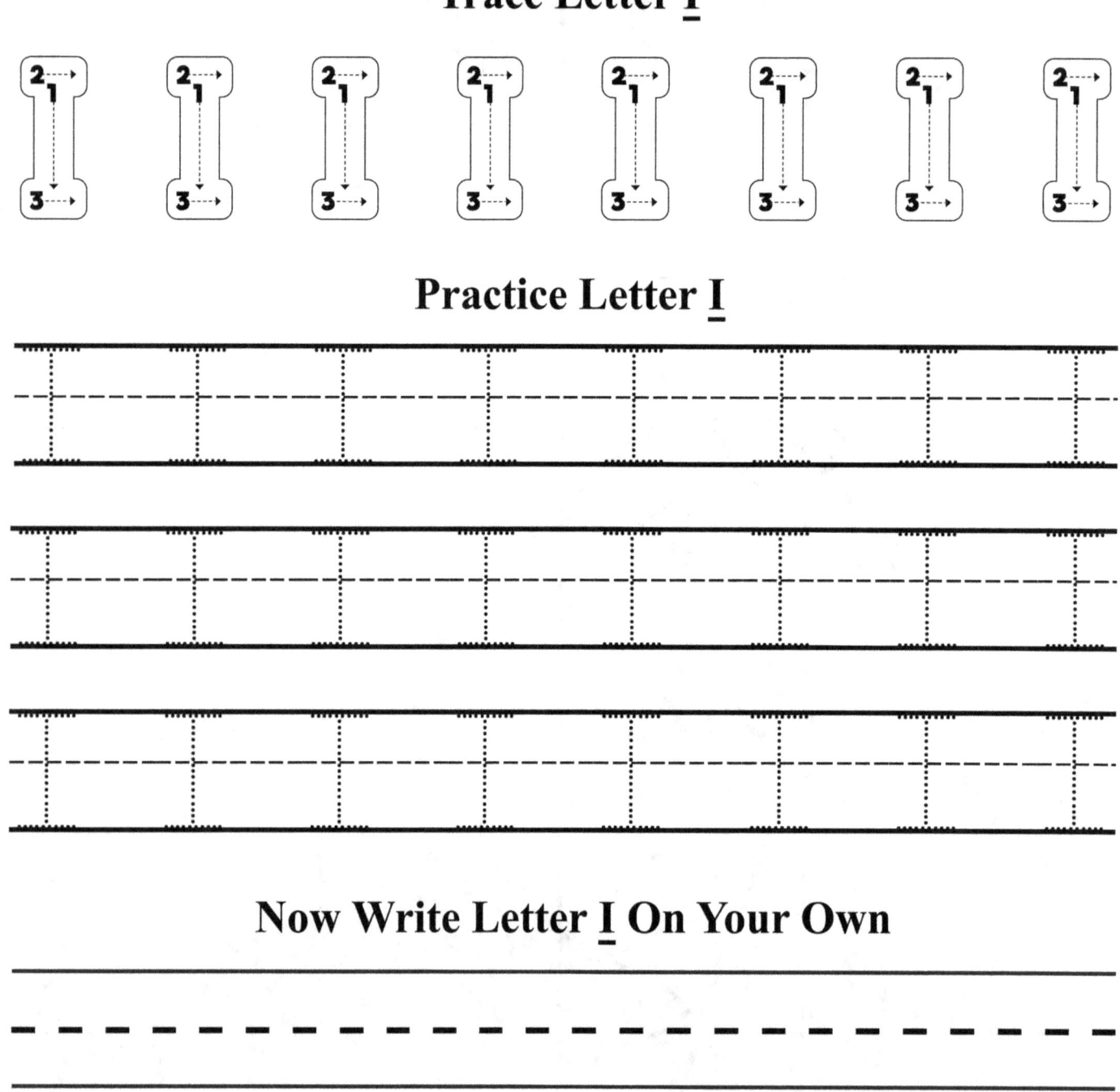

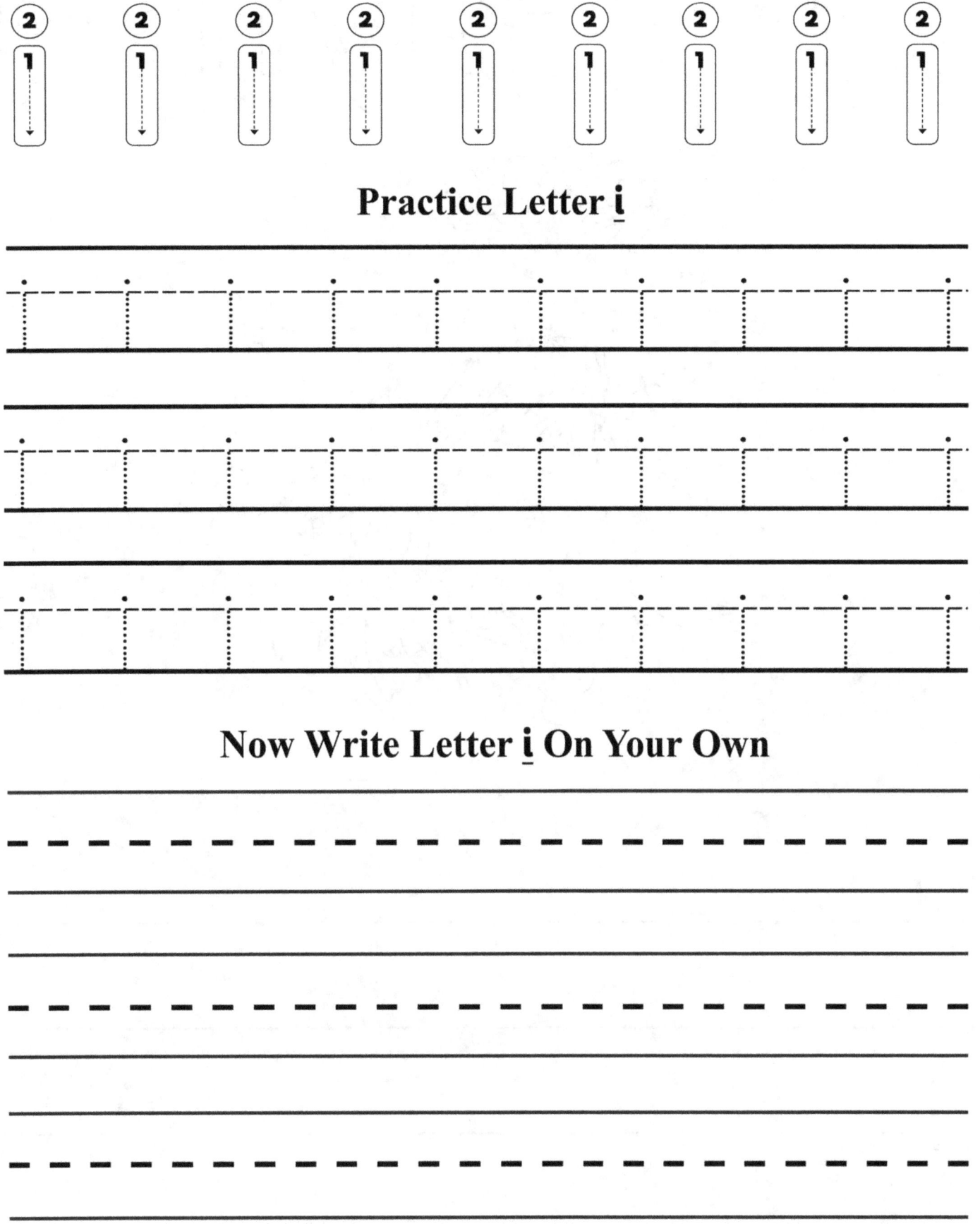

Jj Jellyfish

J _____

j _____

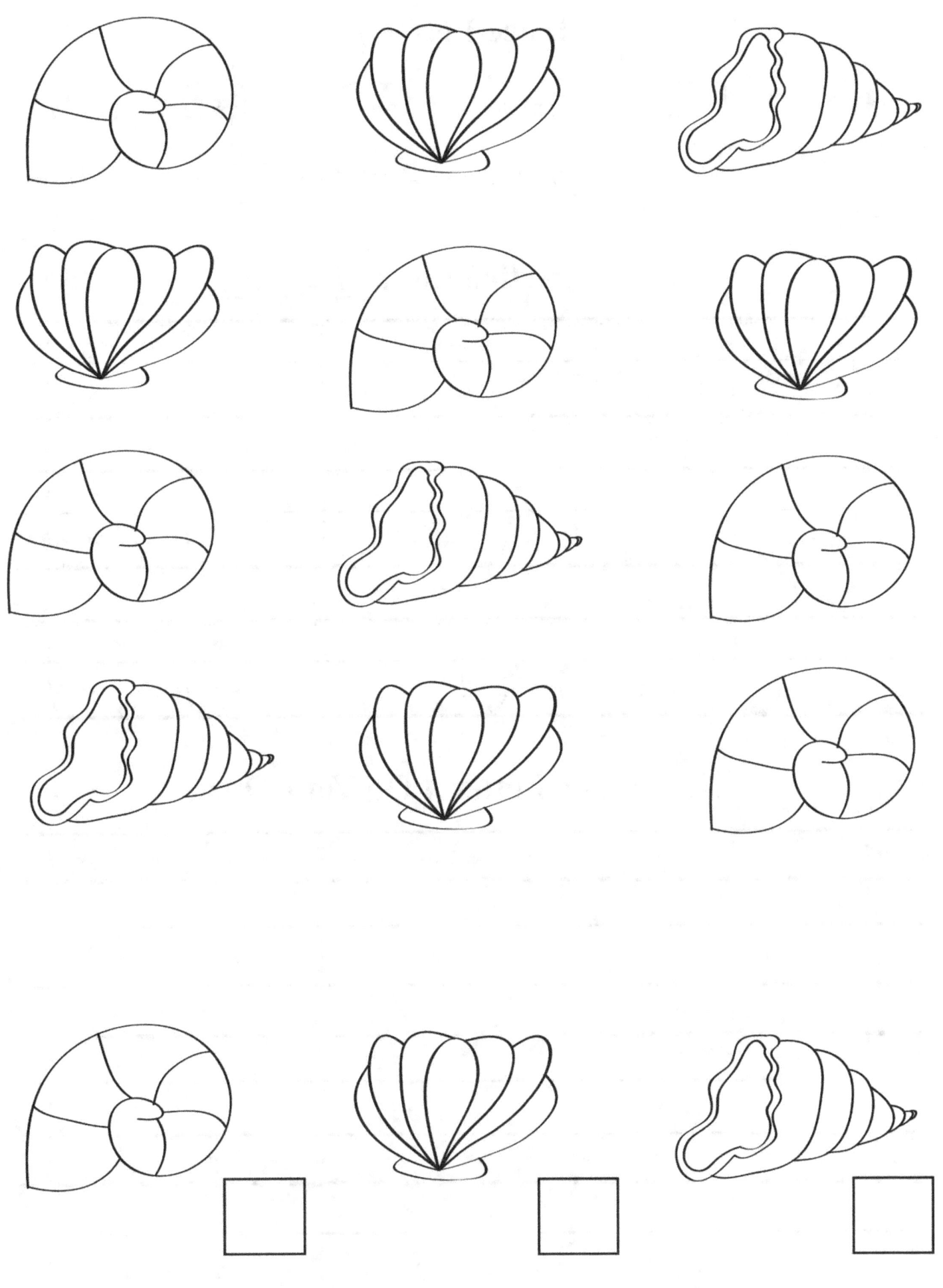

Trace Letter J

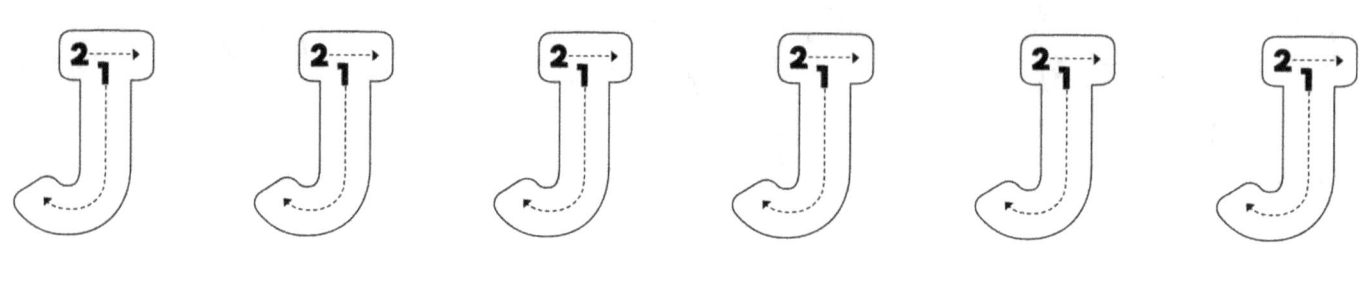

Practice Letter J

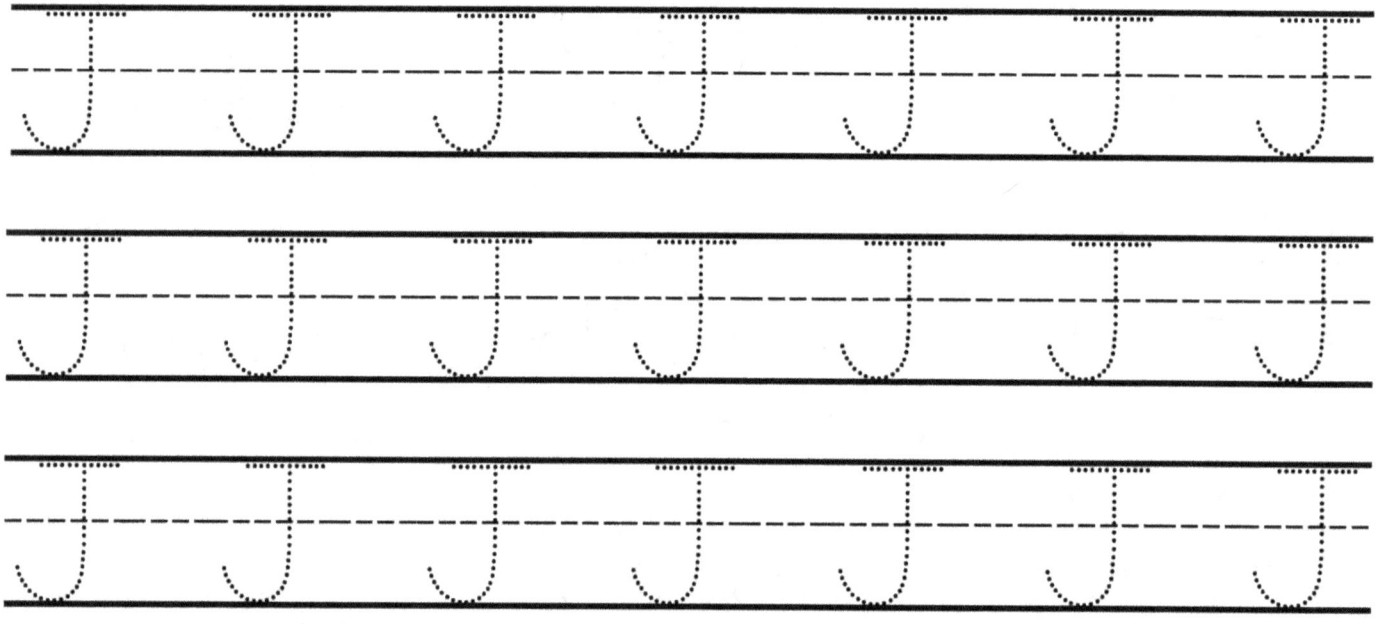

Now Write Letter J On Your Own

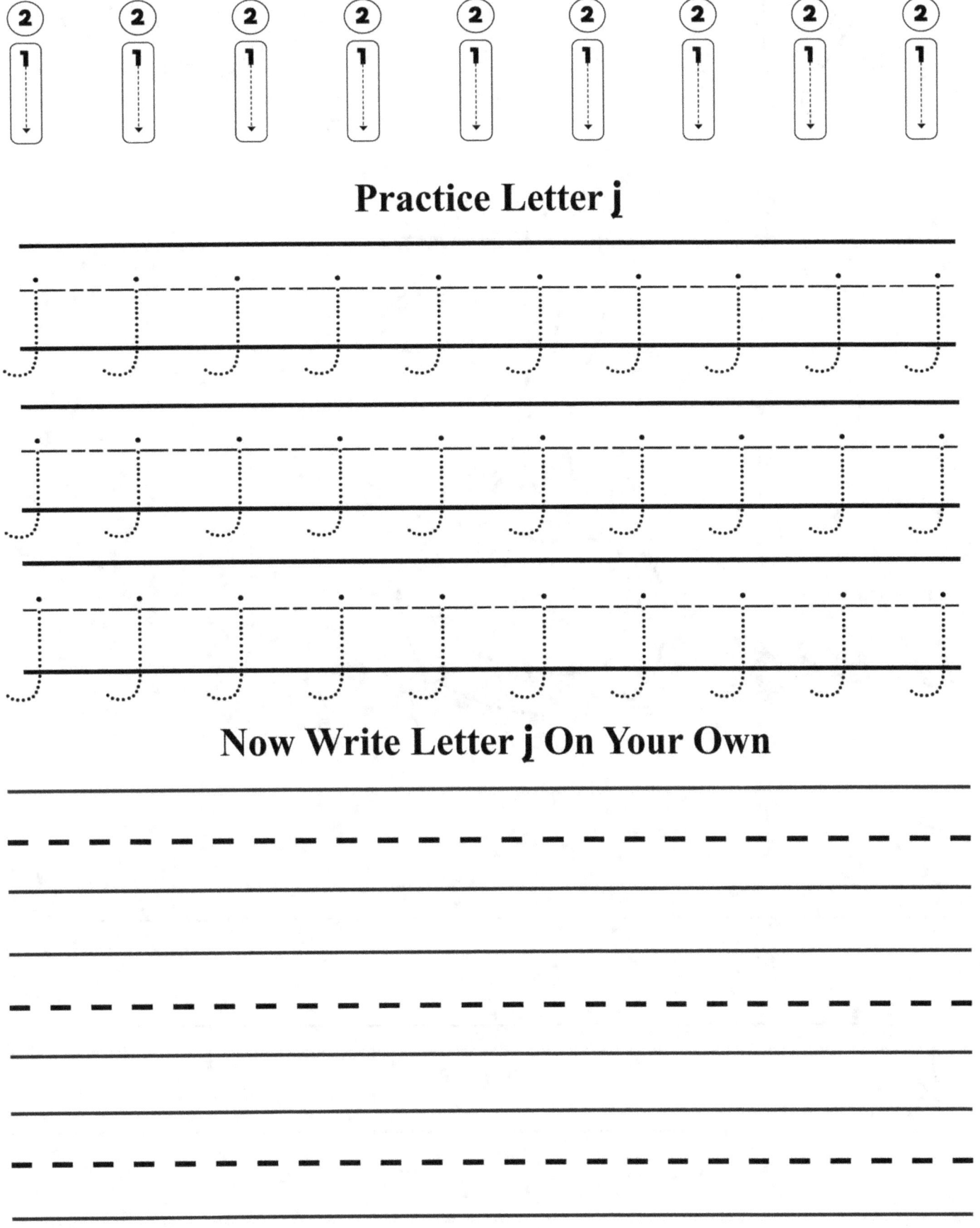

Kk   Key

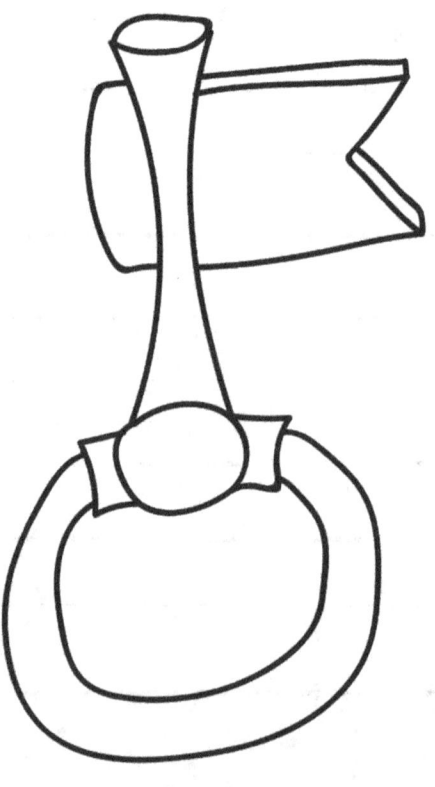

K _____

k _____

Trace Letter K

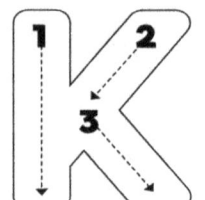 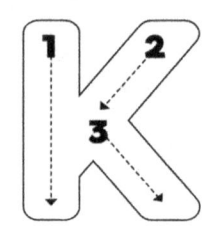 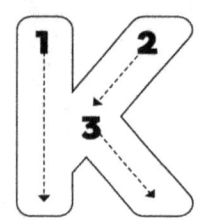 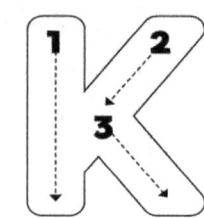 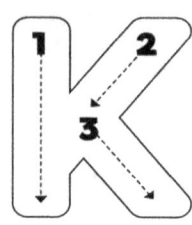

Practice Letter K

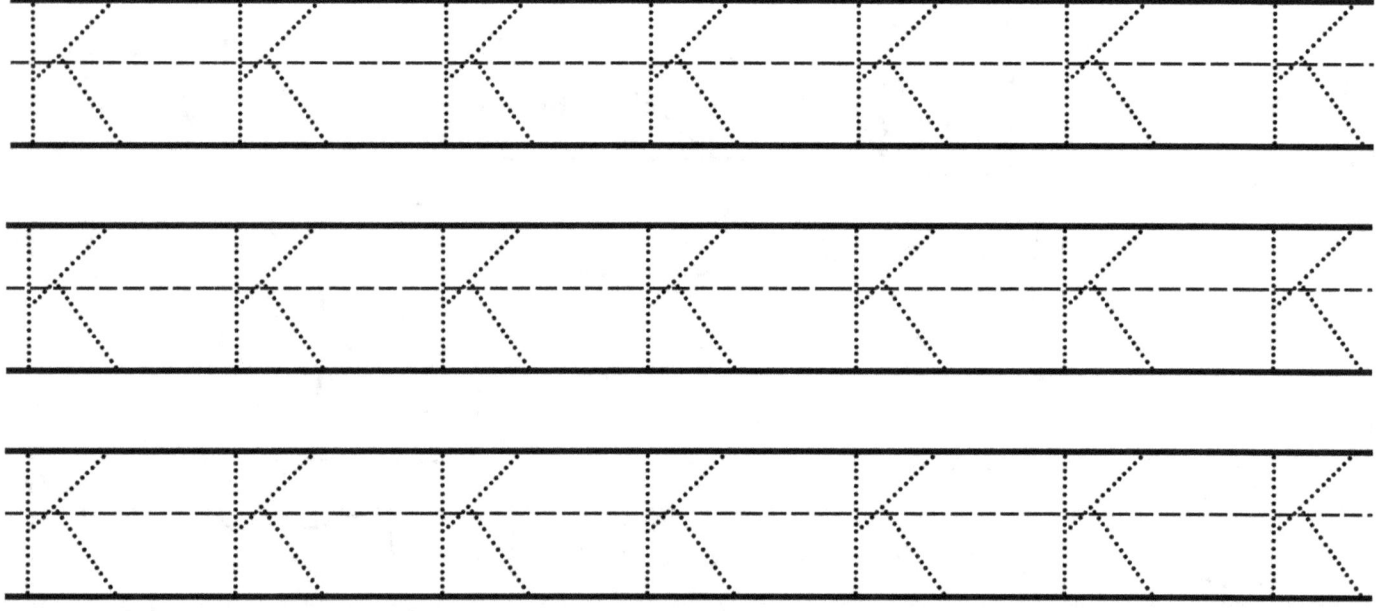

Now Write Letter K On Your Own

Trace Letter k

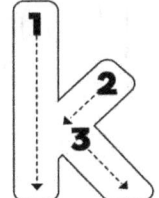 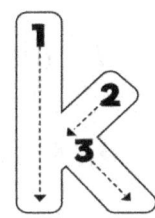 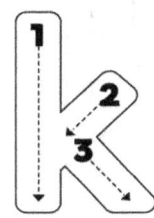 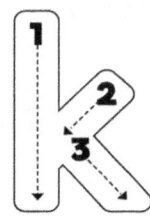 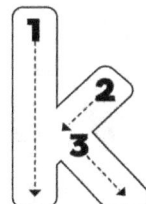 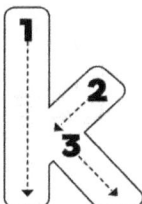

Practice Letter k

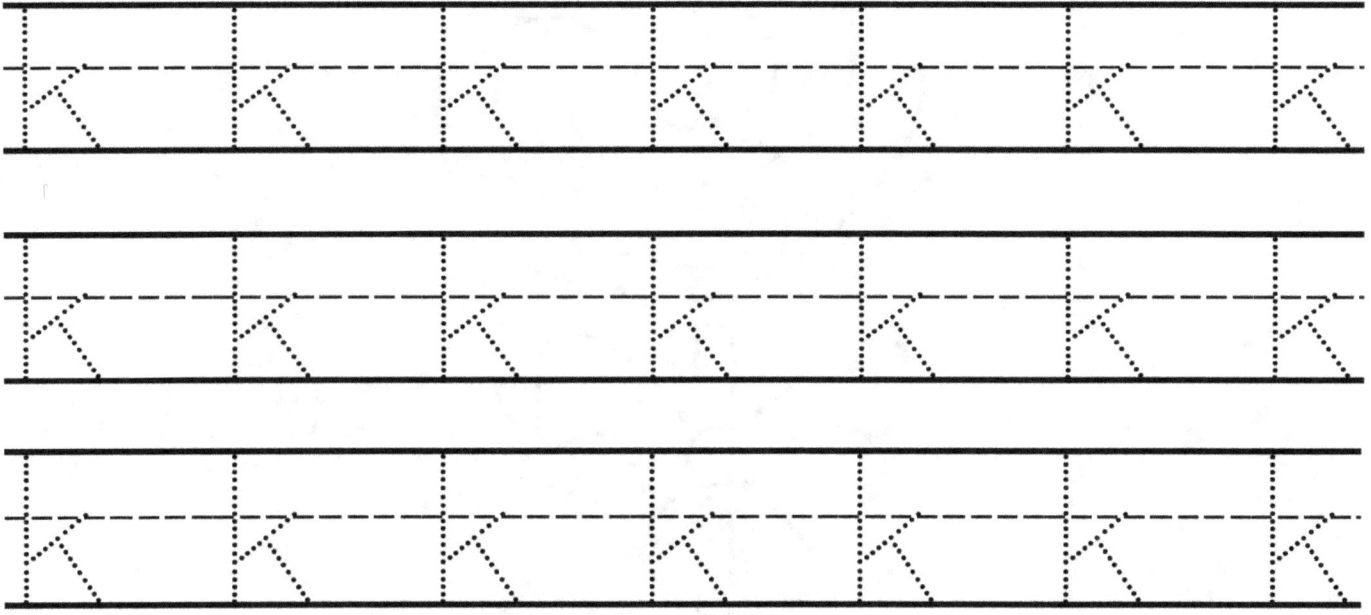

Now Write Letter k On Your Own

Ll Lollipop

L _____

l _____

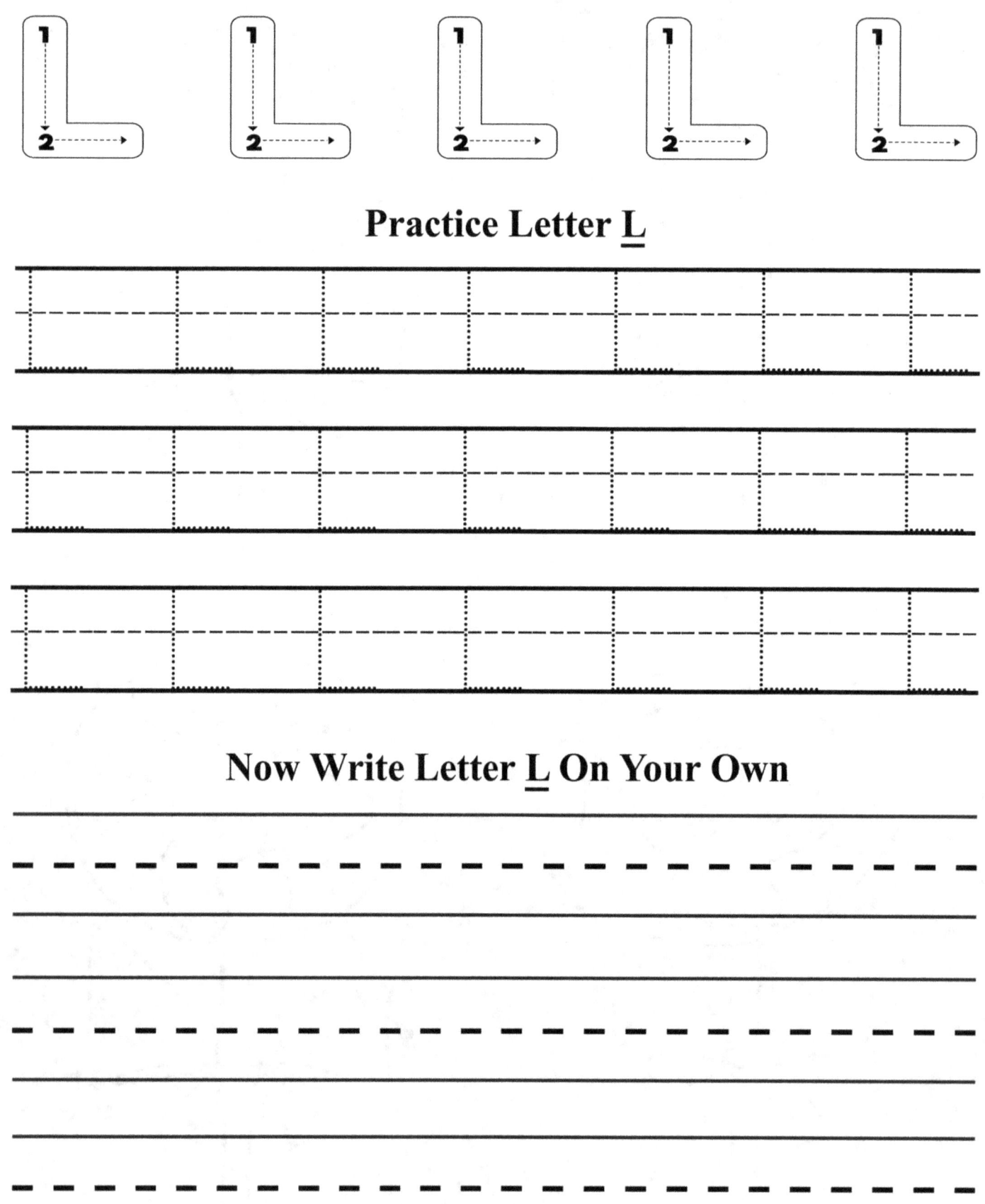

Trace Letter l

Practice Letter l

Now Write Letter l On Your Own

Mm Mouse

M _____

m _____

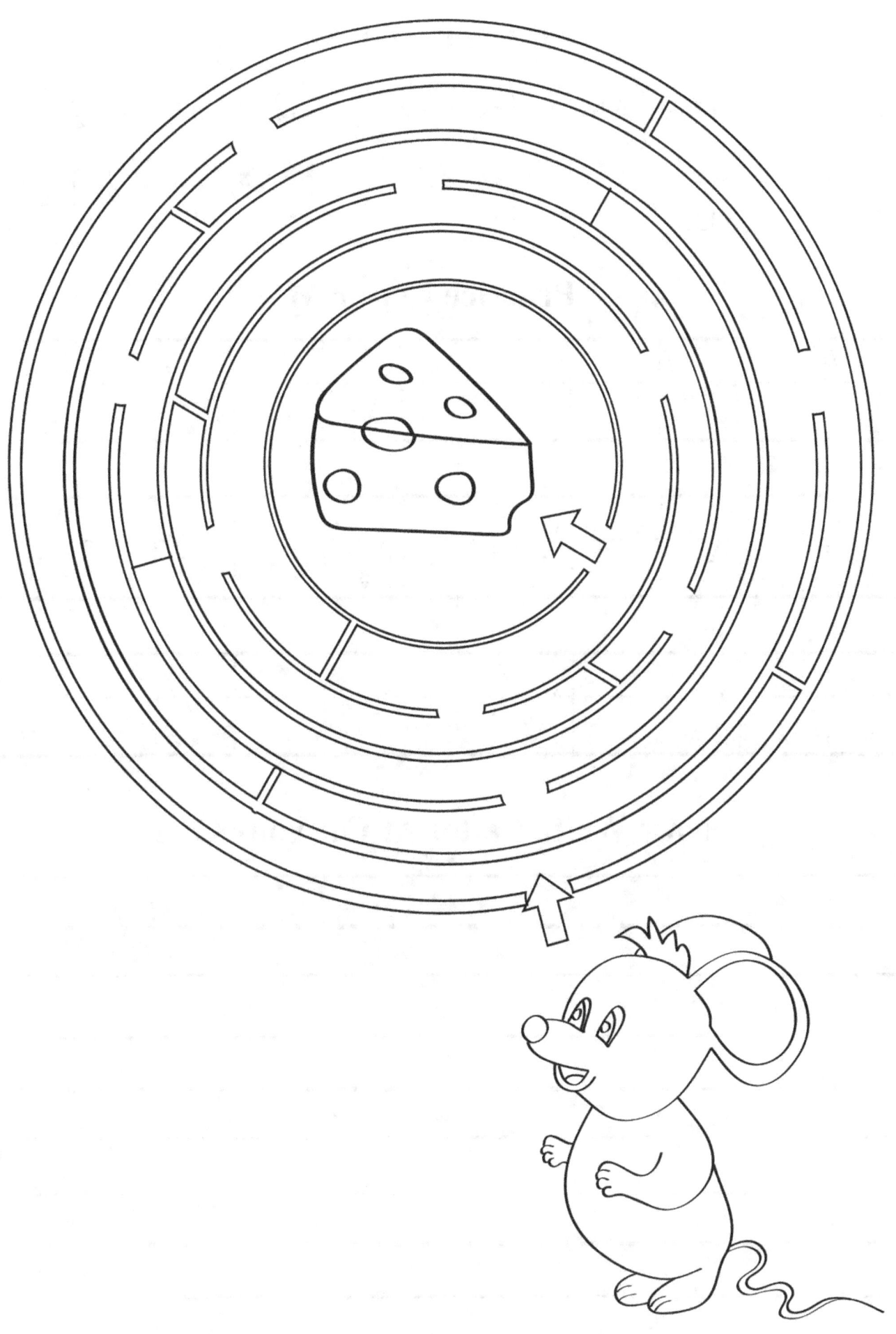

Trace Letter M

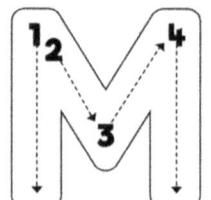 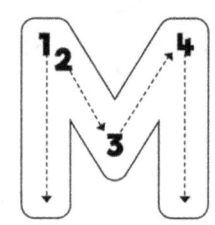 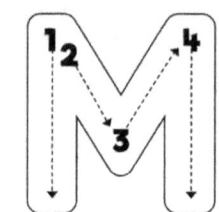 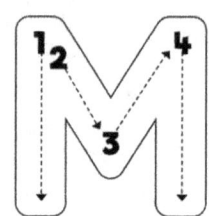 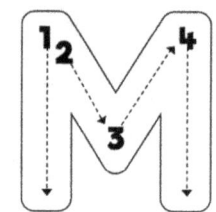

Practice Letter M

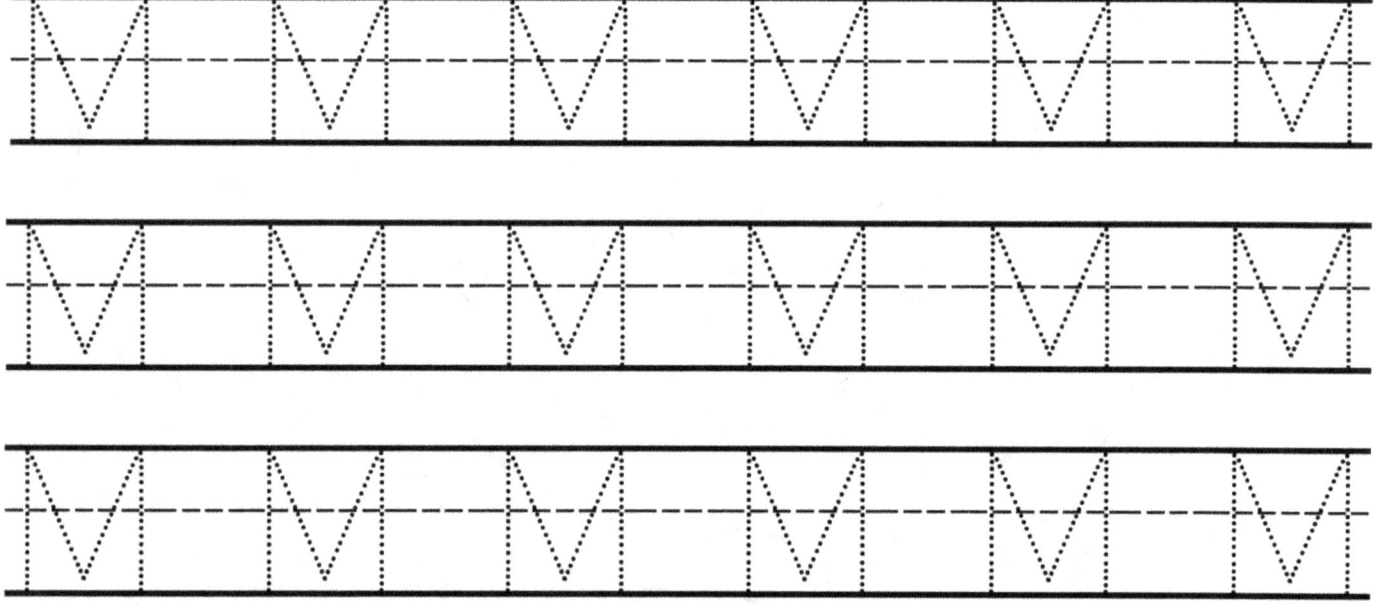

Now Write Letter M On Your Own

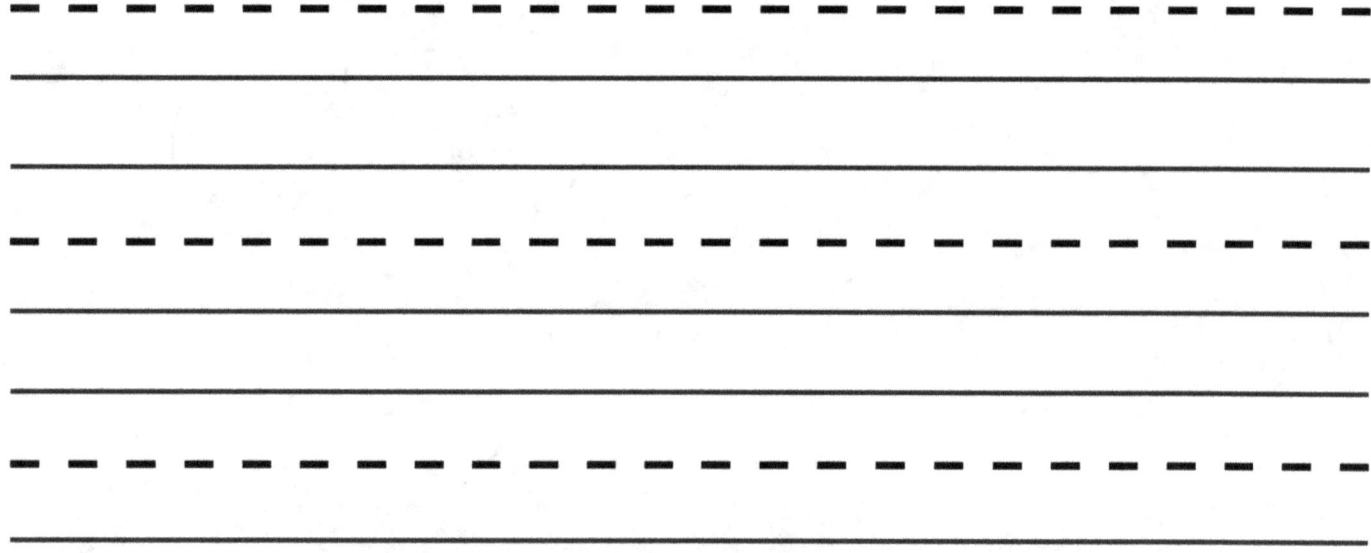

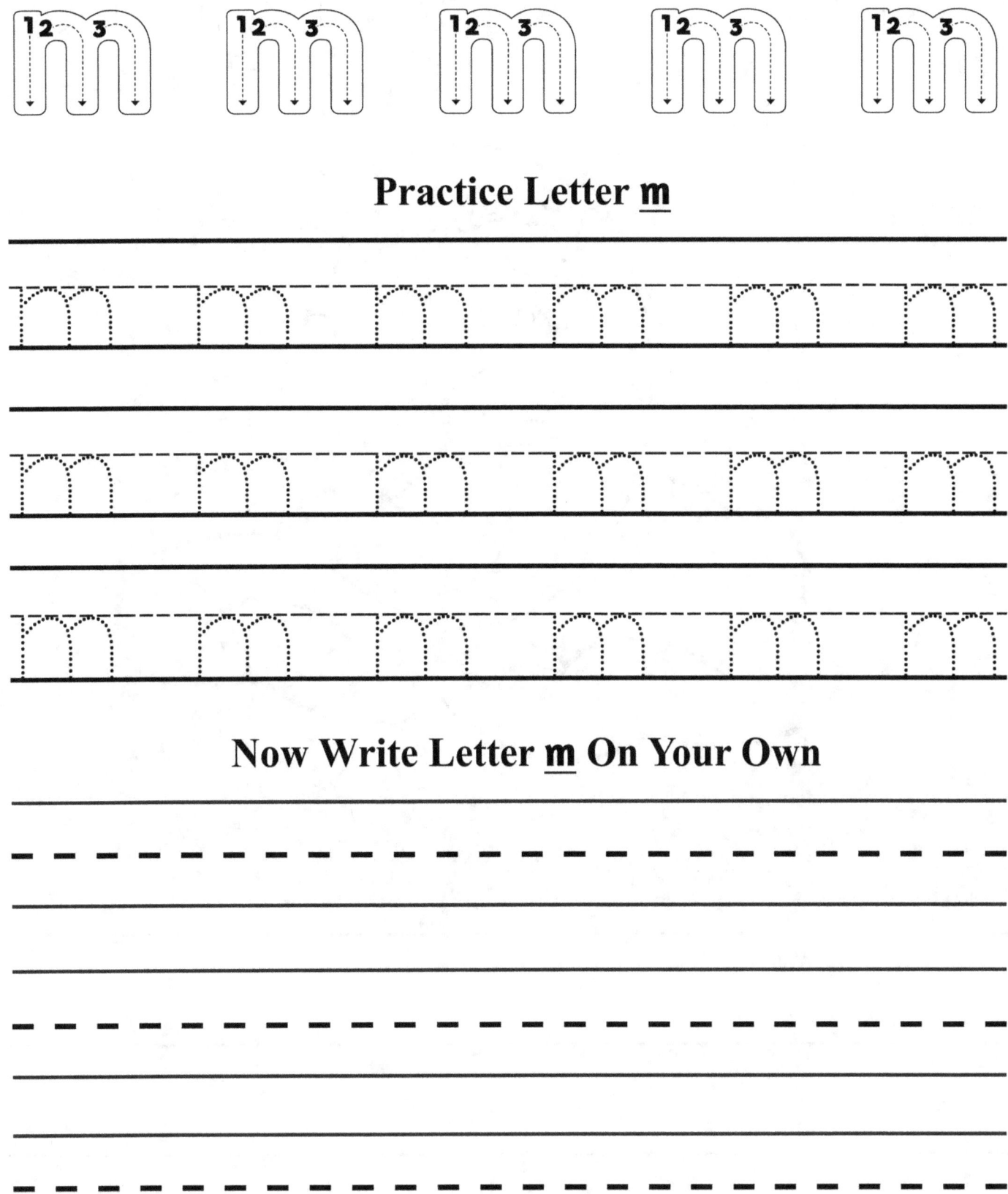

Nn Night

N _____

n _____

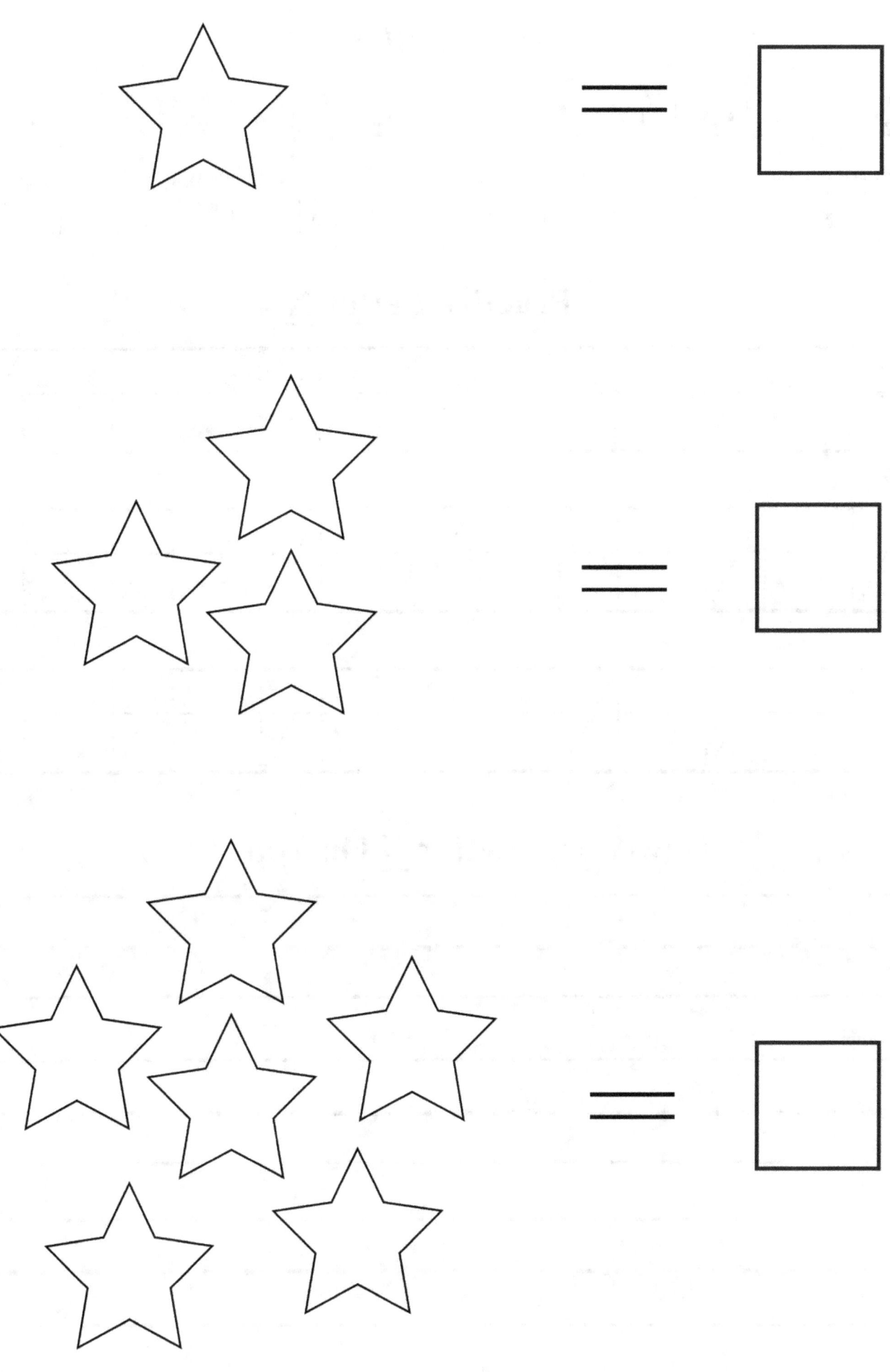

Trace Letter N

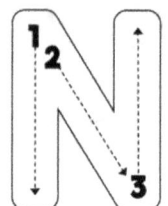 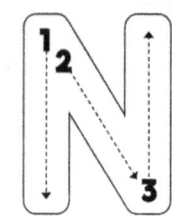 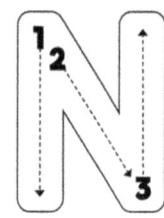 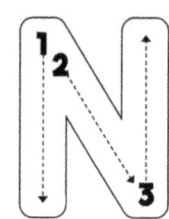 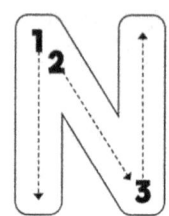 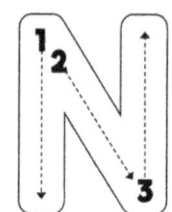

Practice Letter N

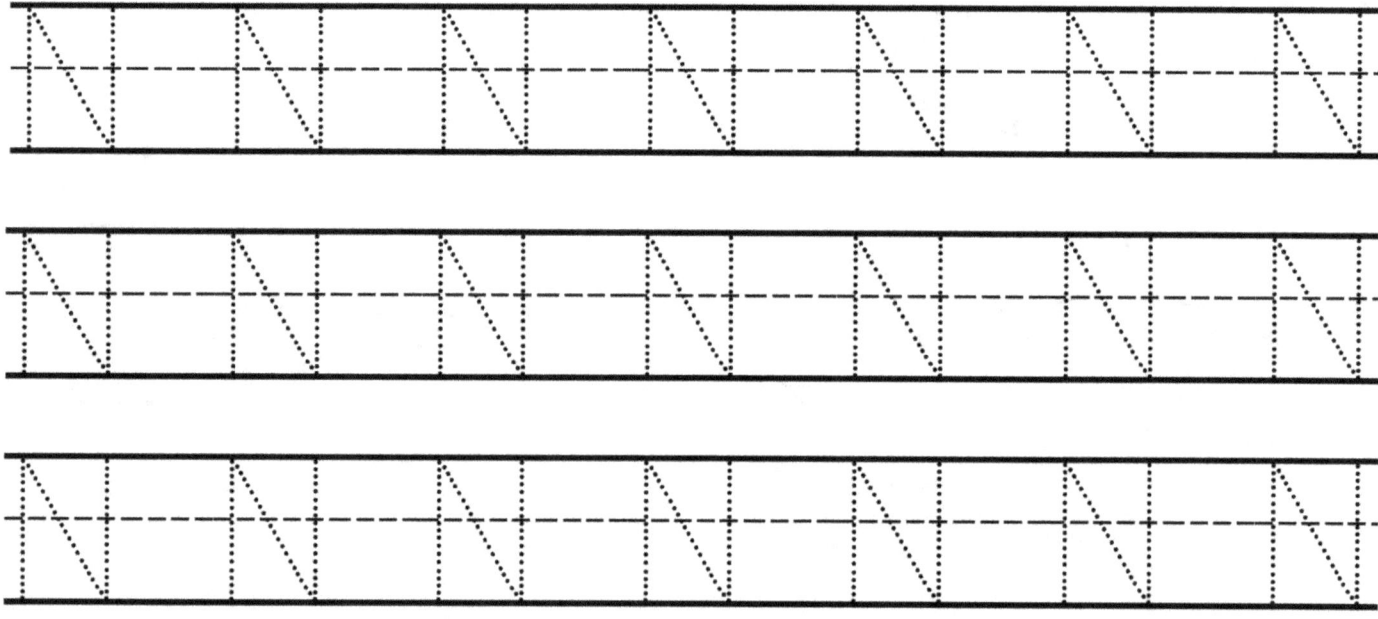

Now Write Letter N On Your Own

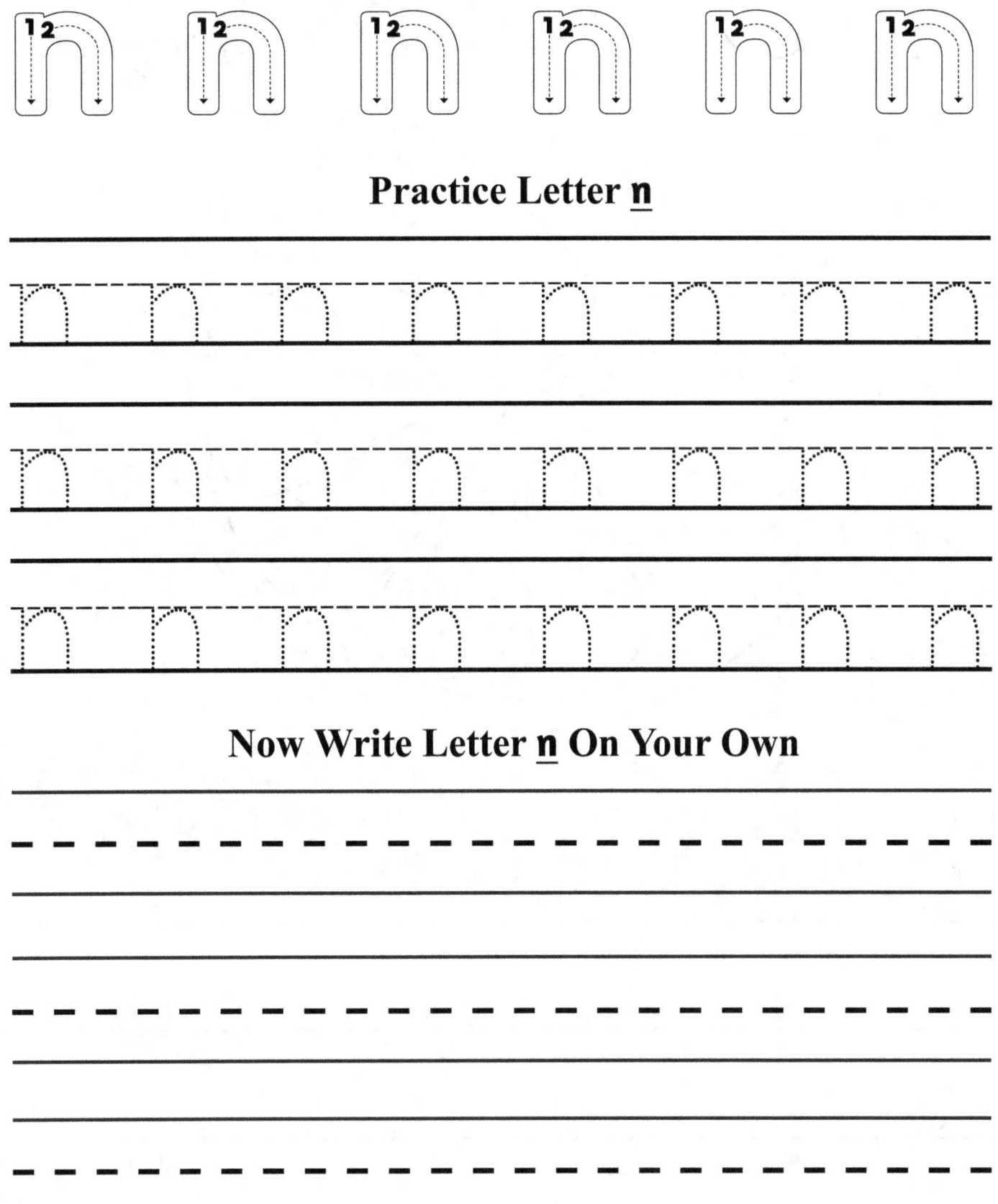

Oo Orange

O _____

o _____

Trace Letter O

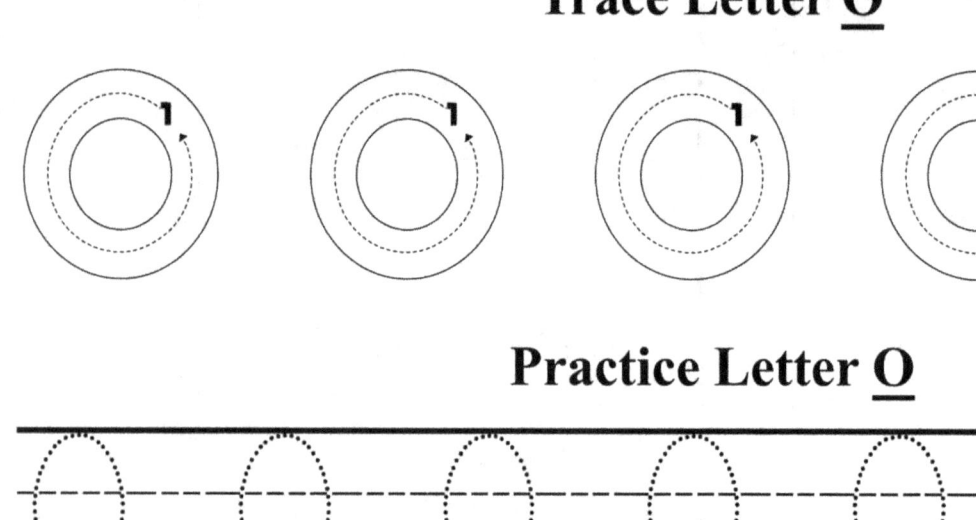

Practice Letter O

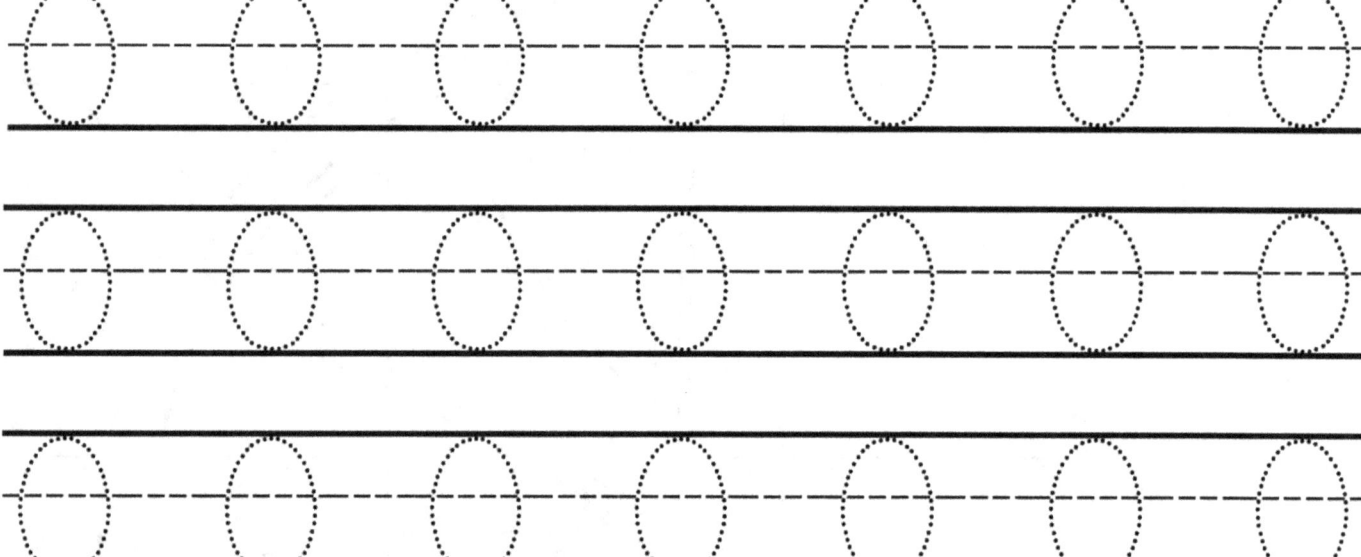

Now Write Letter O On Your Own

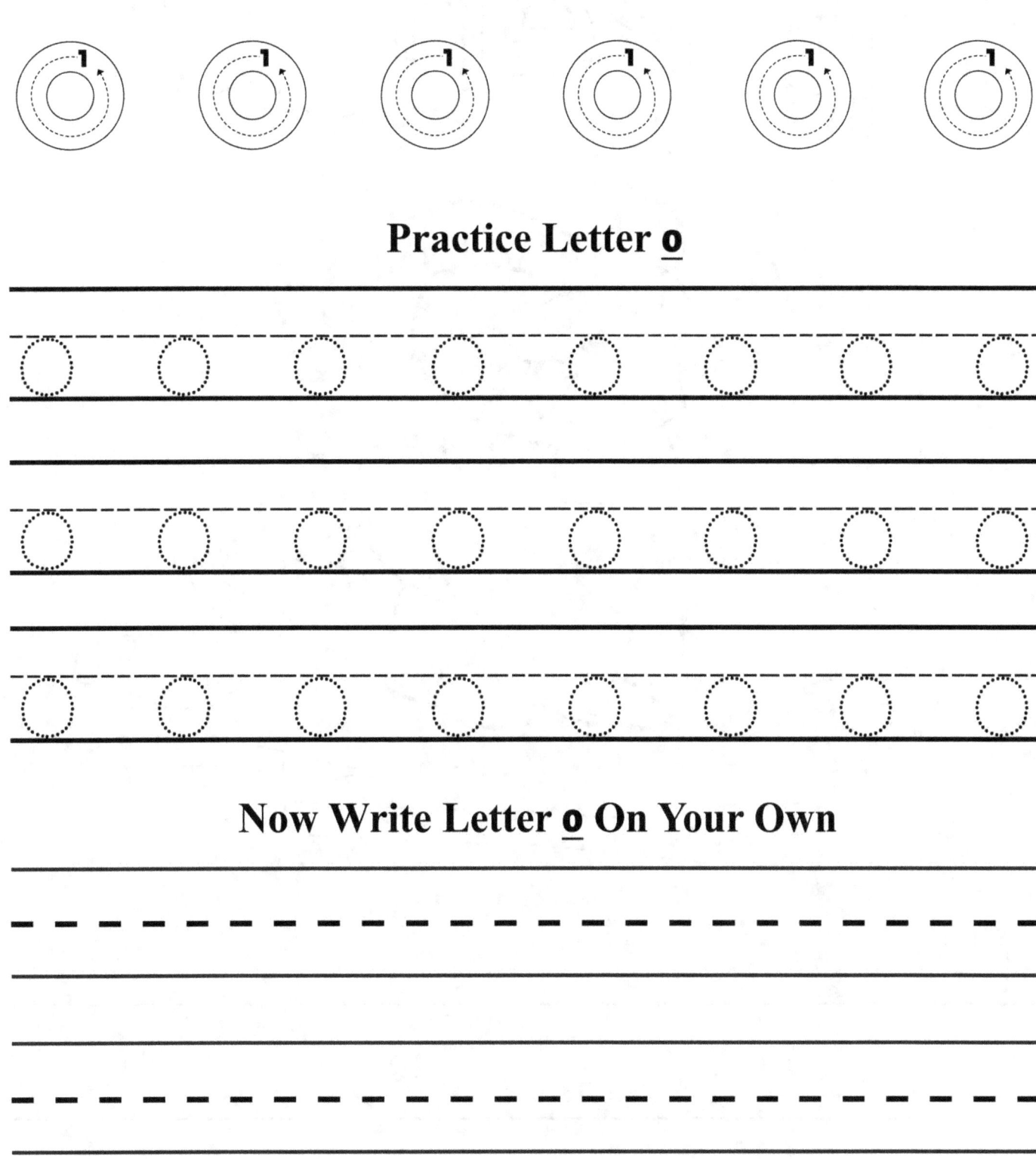

Pp Penguin

P
_____

_____

p
_____

Trace Letter P

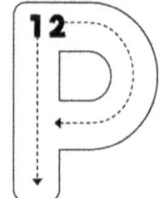 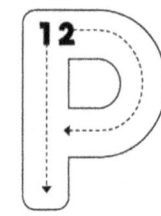 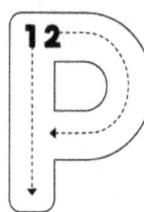 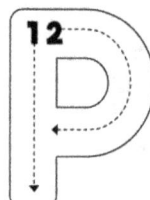 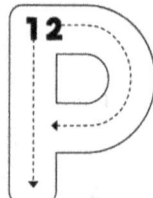 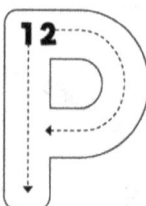

Practice Letter P

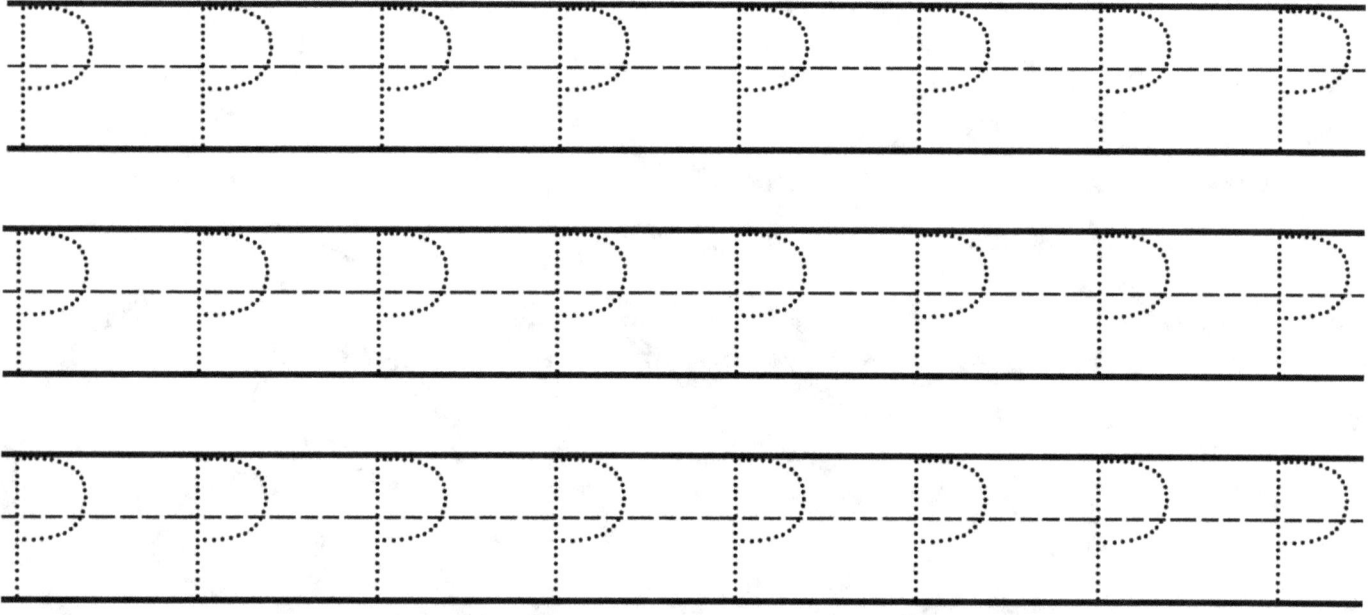

Now Write Letter P On Your Own

Trace Letter p

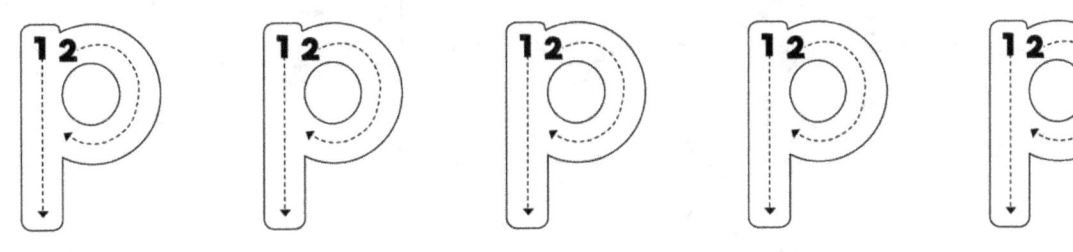

Practice Letter p

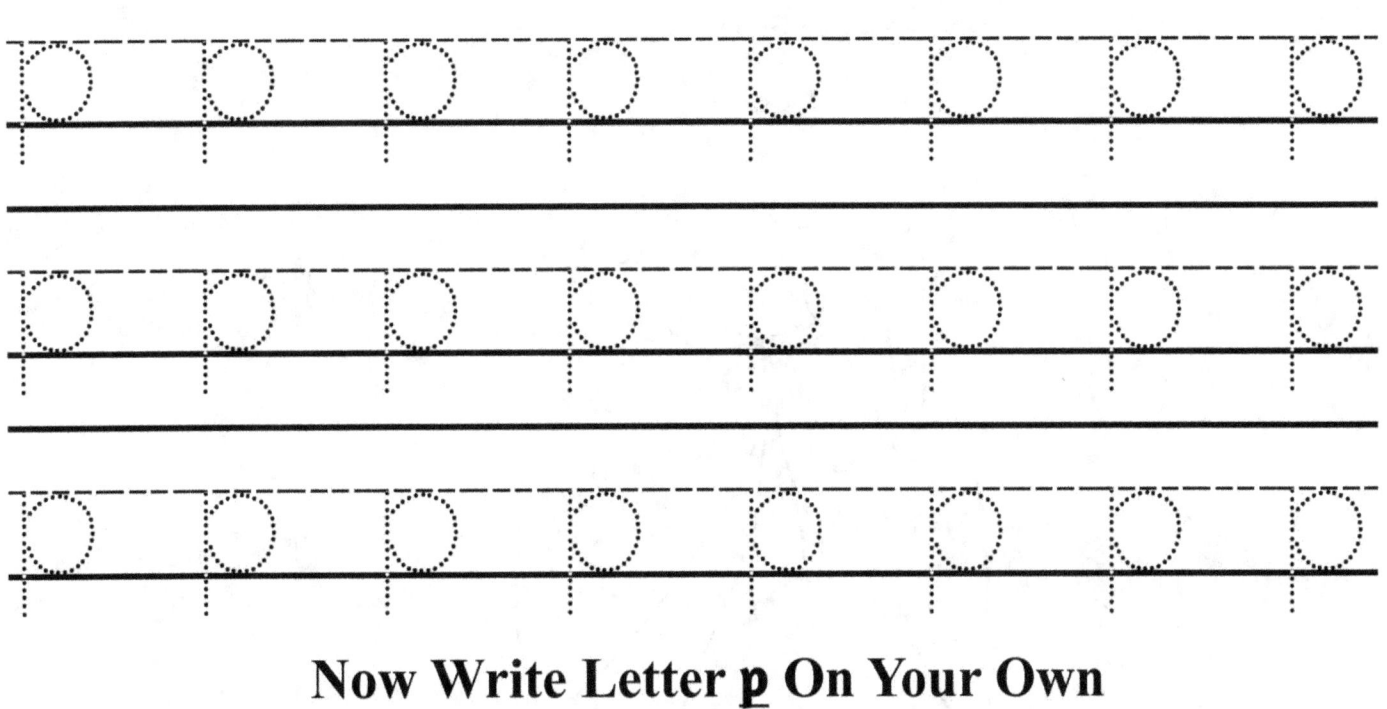

Now Write Letter p On Your Own

Qq Queen

Q _____

q _____

Trace Letter Q

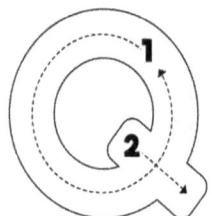 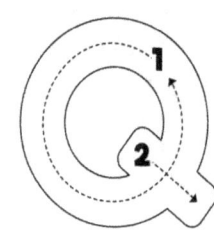 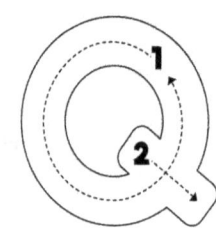 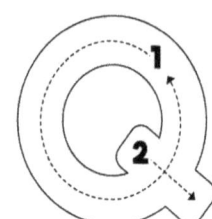 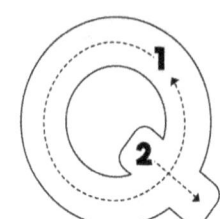

Practice Letter Q

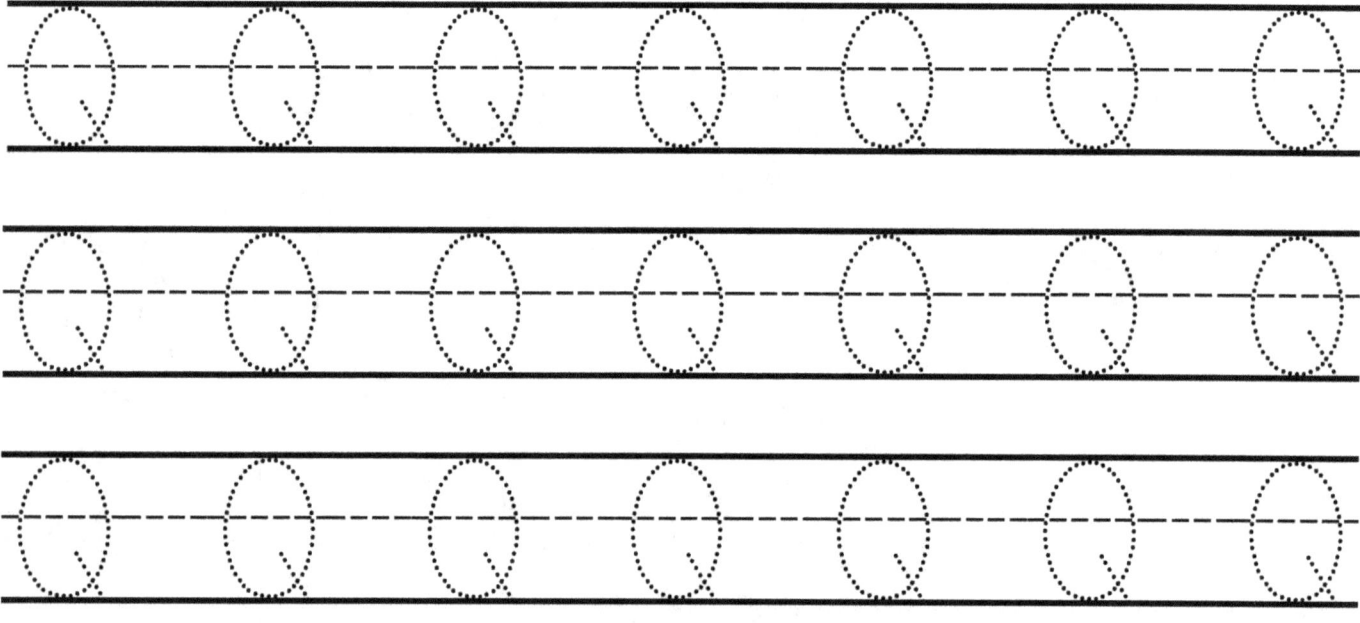

Now Write Letter Q On Your Own

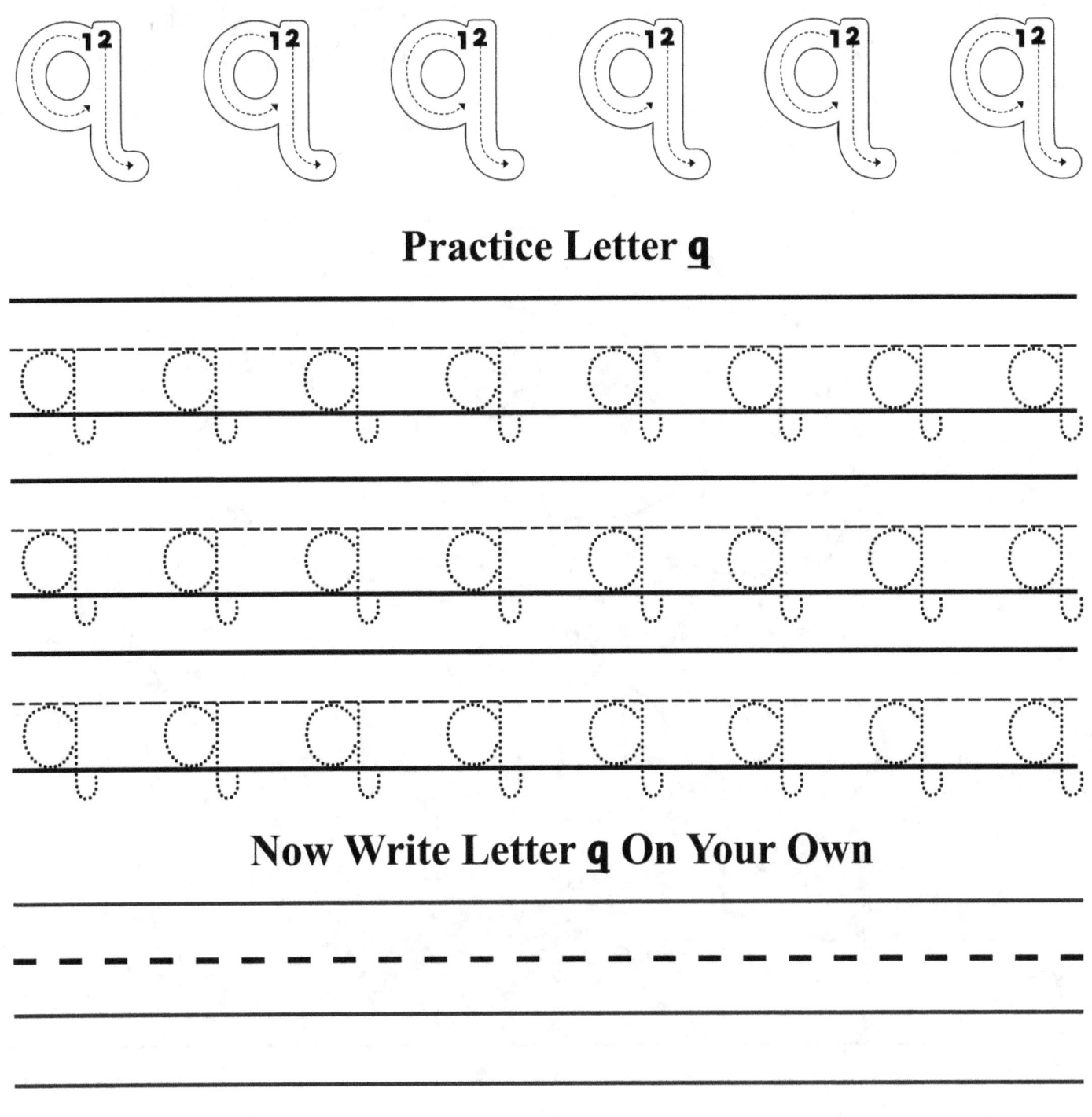

Rr Rain

R _____

r _____

Trace Letter R

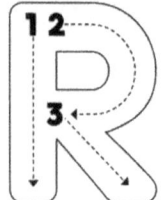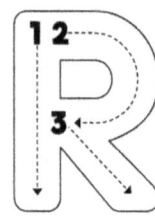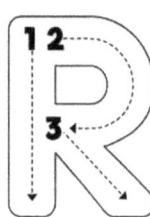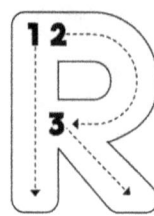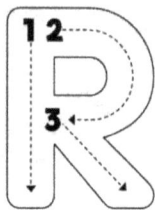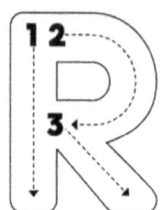

Practice Letter R

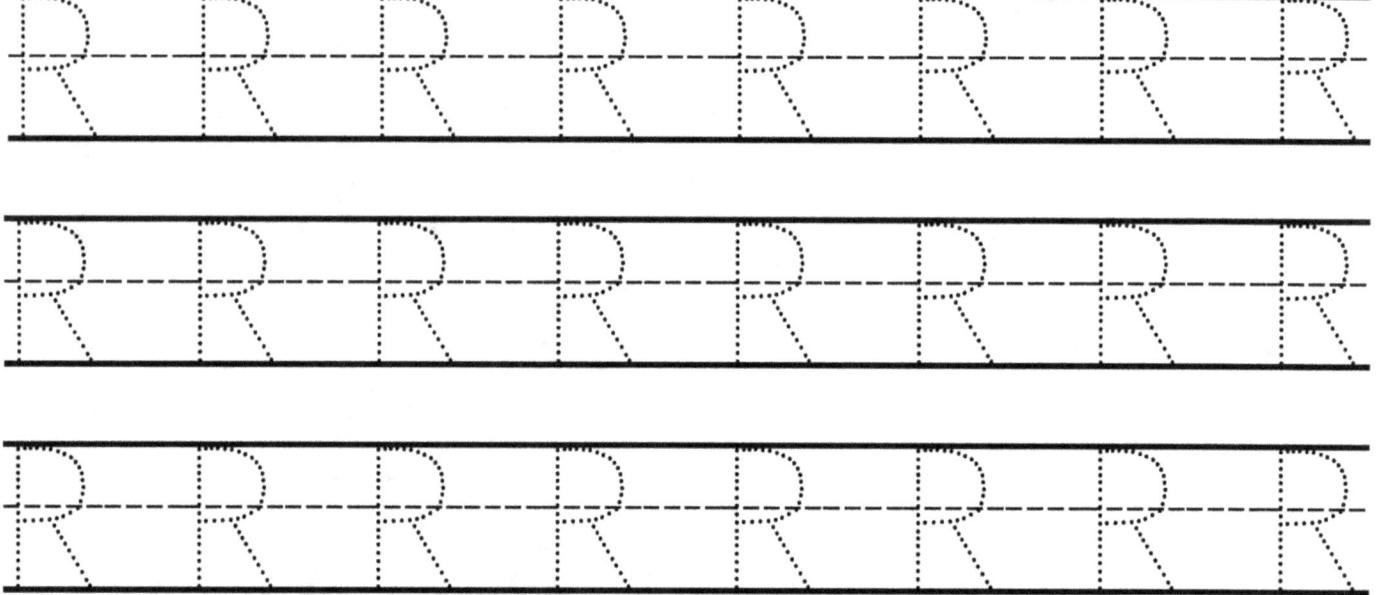

Now Write Letter R On Your Own

Trace Letter r

Practice Letter r

Now Write Letter r On Your Own

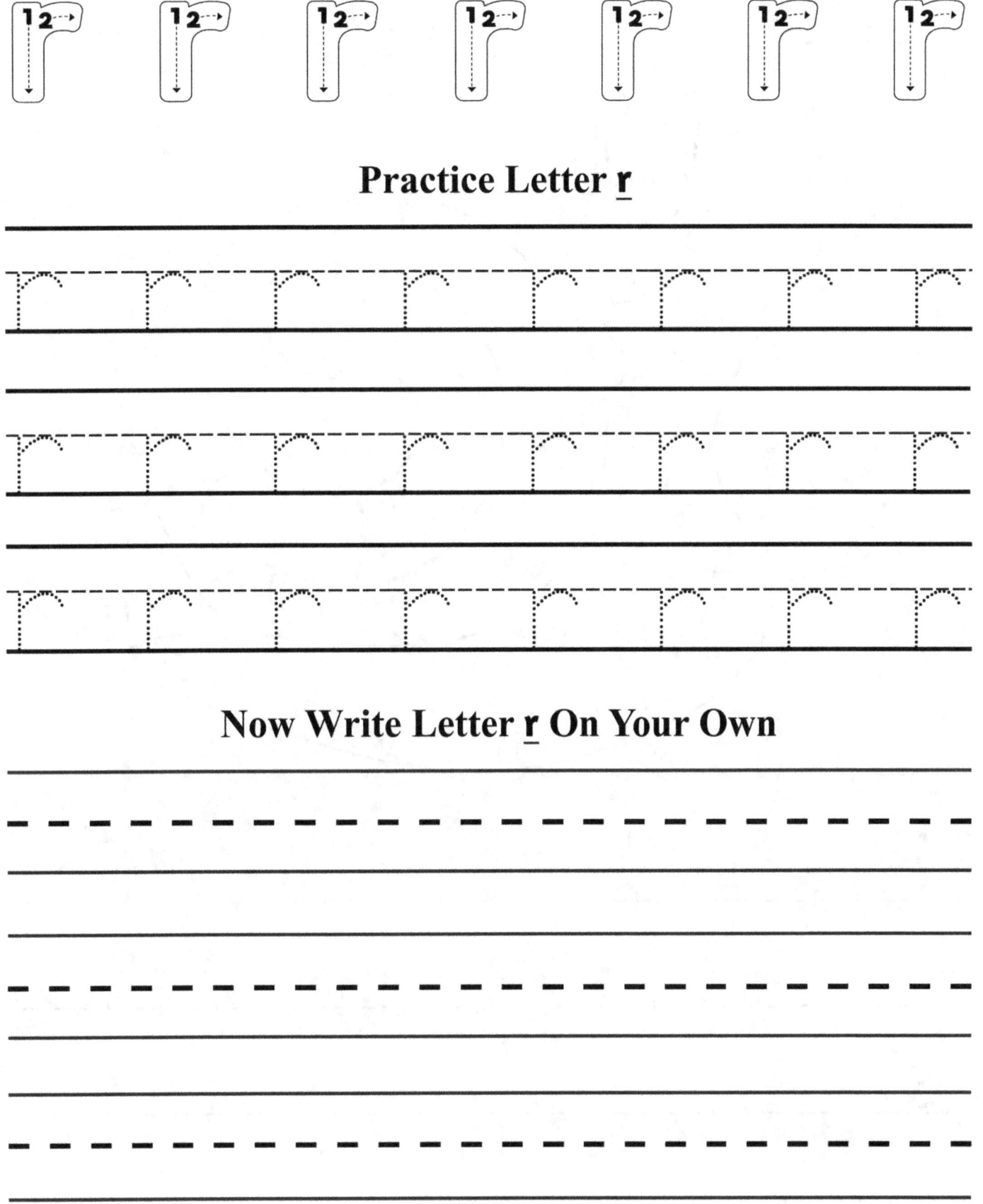

S s   Snail

S
_____

s
_____

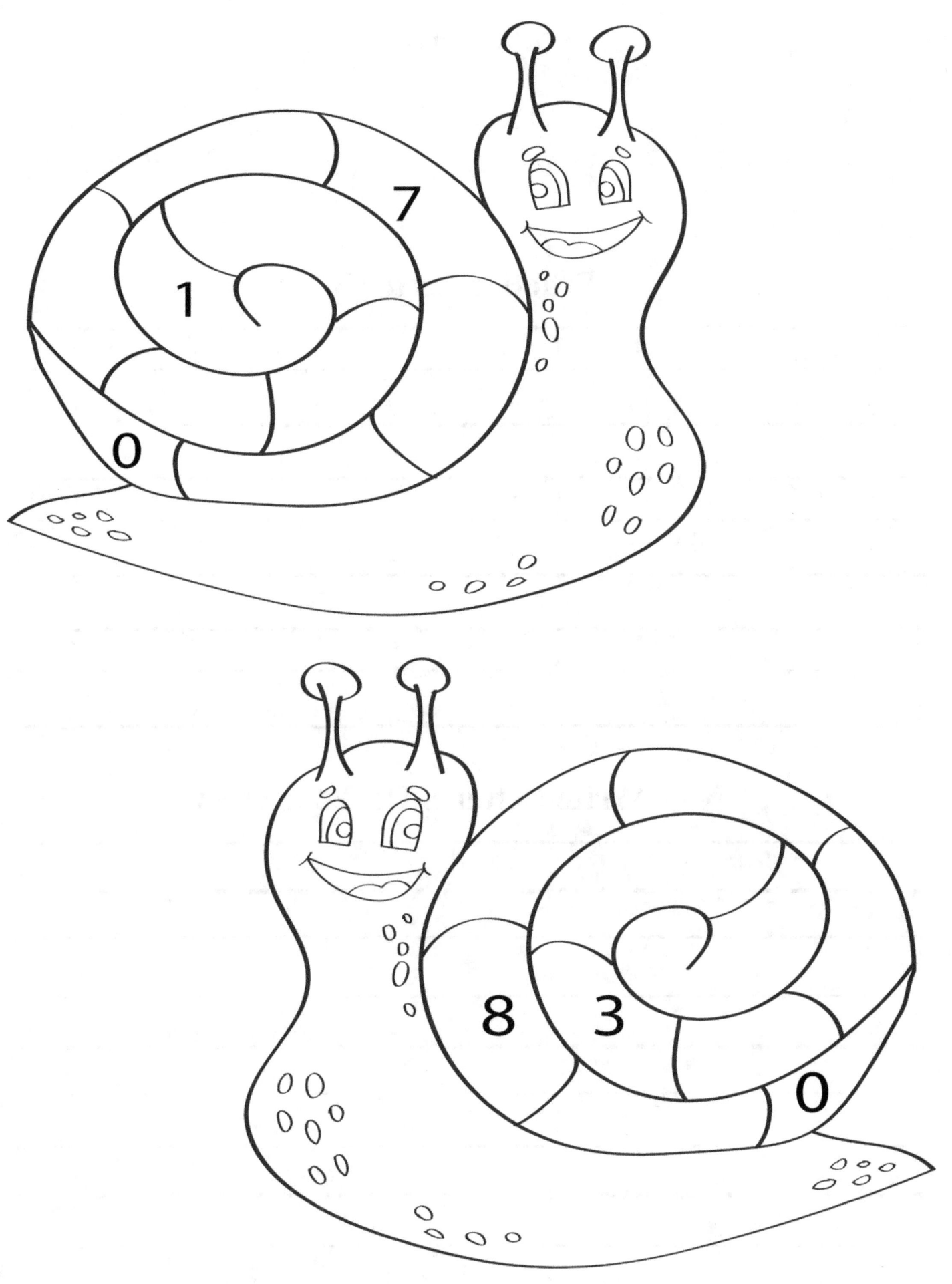

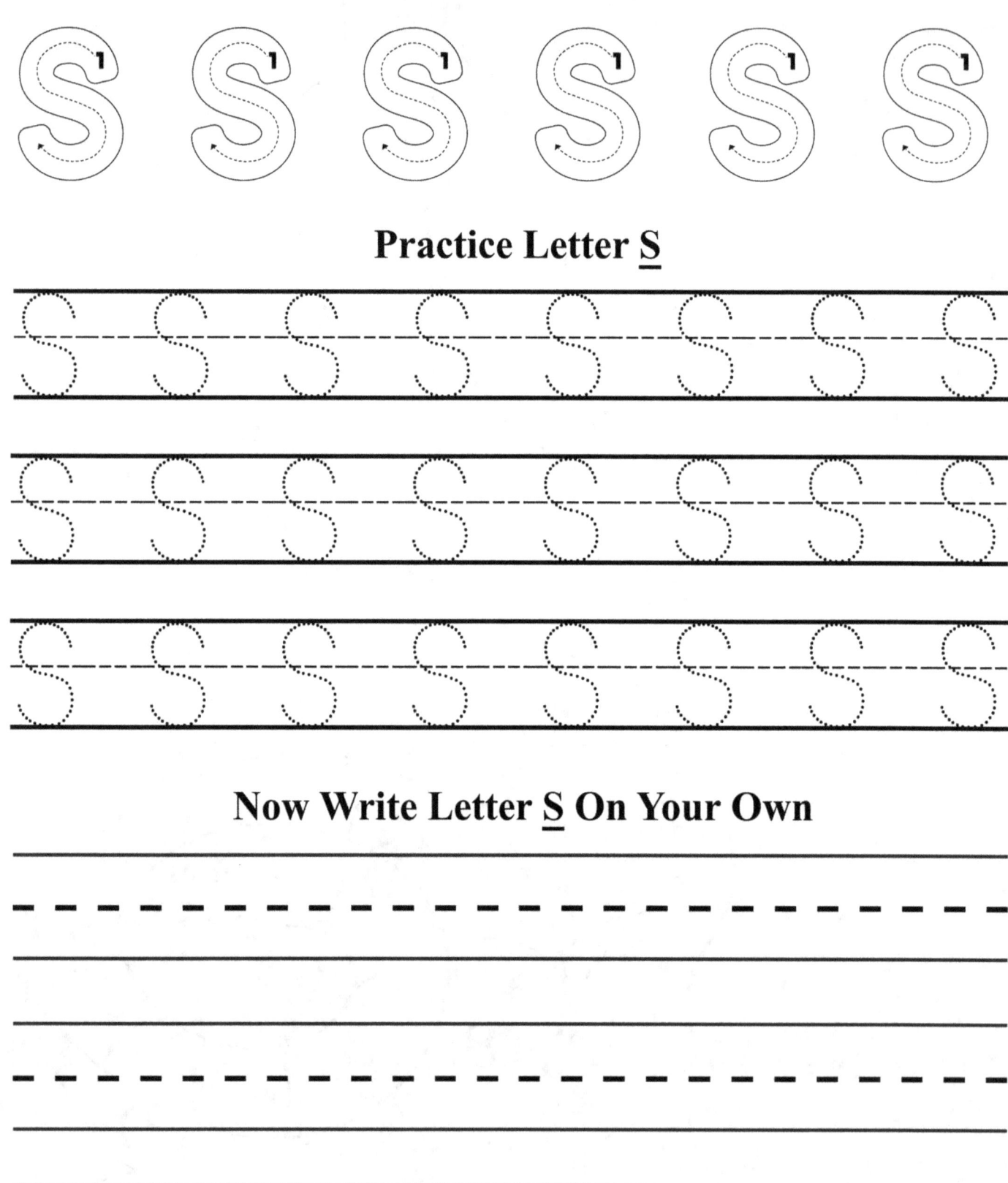

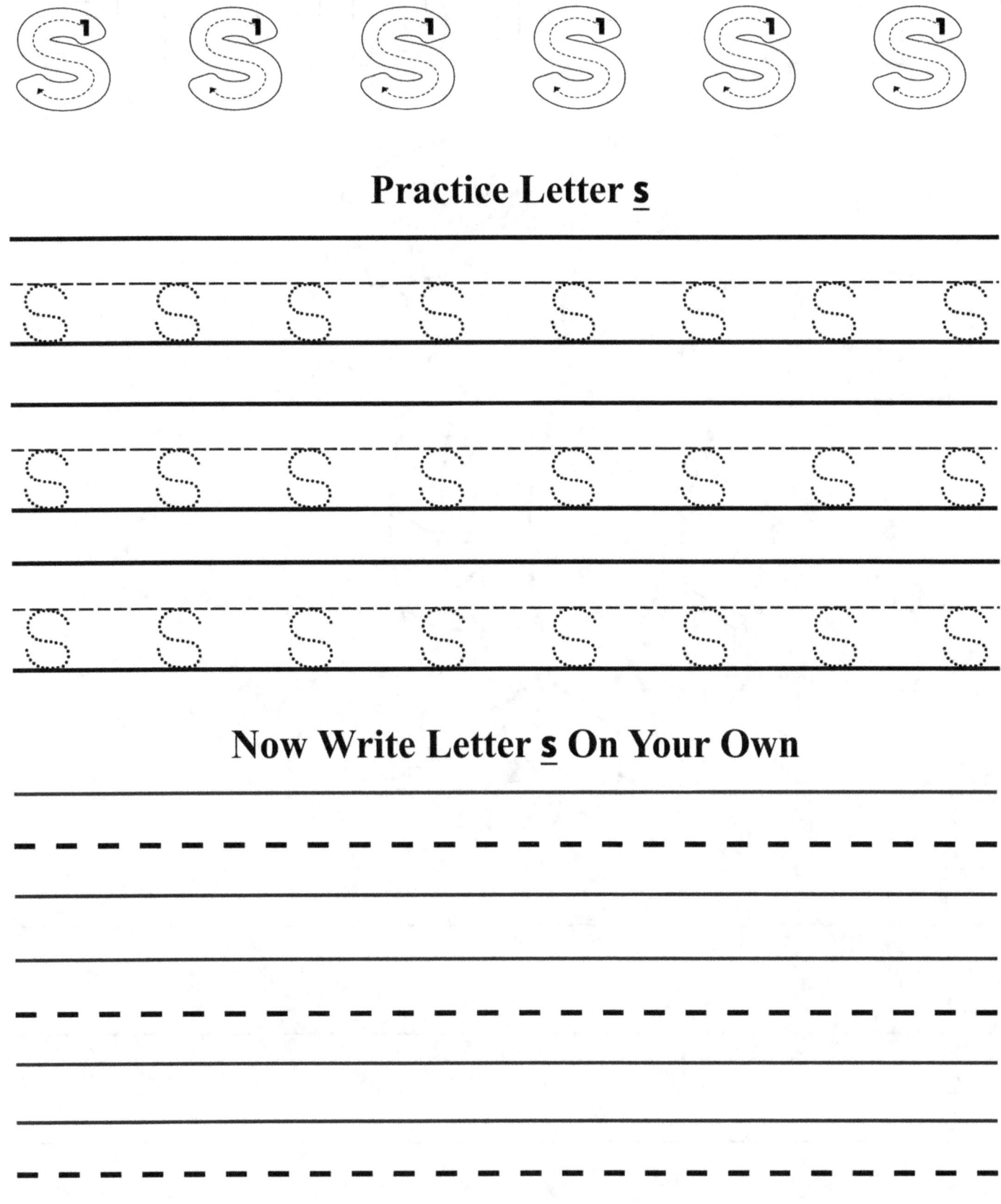

Tt Turtle

T _____

_____

t _____

_____

Trace Letter T

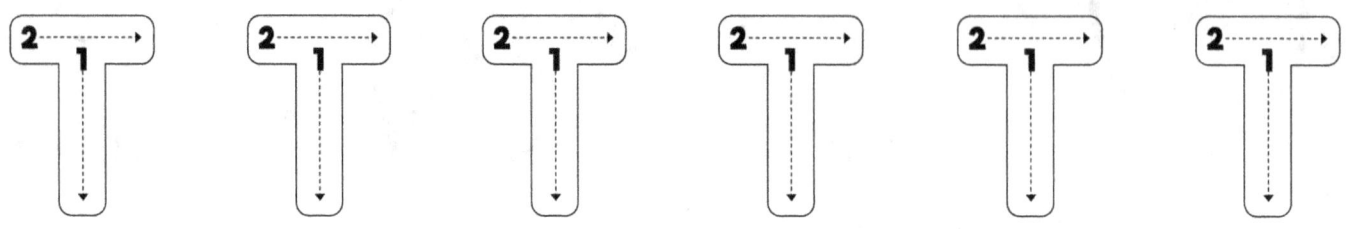

Practice Letter T

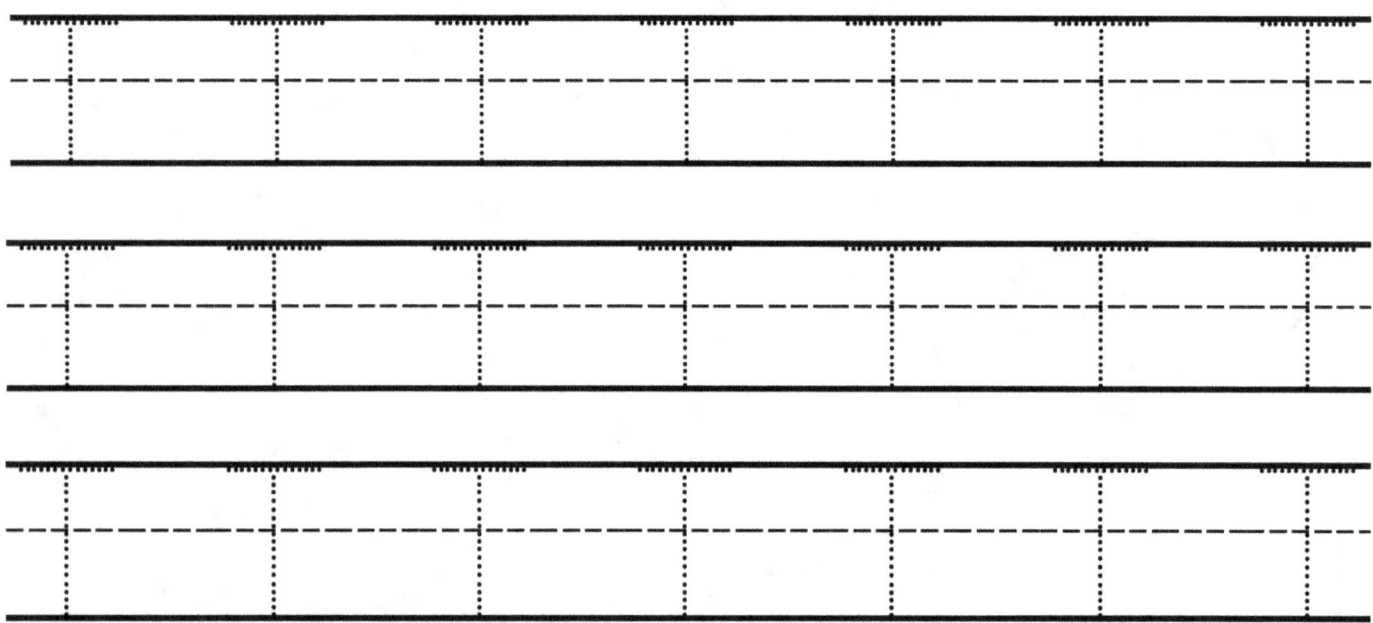

Now Write Letter T On Your Own

Trace Letter t

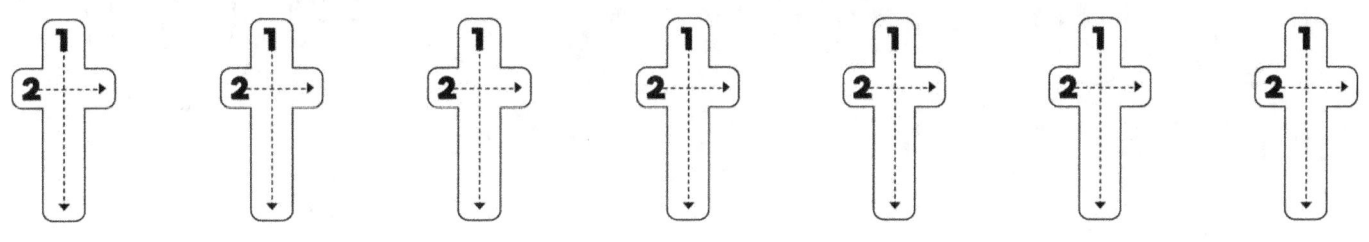

Practice Letter t

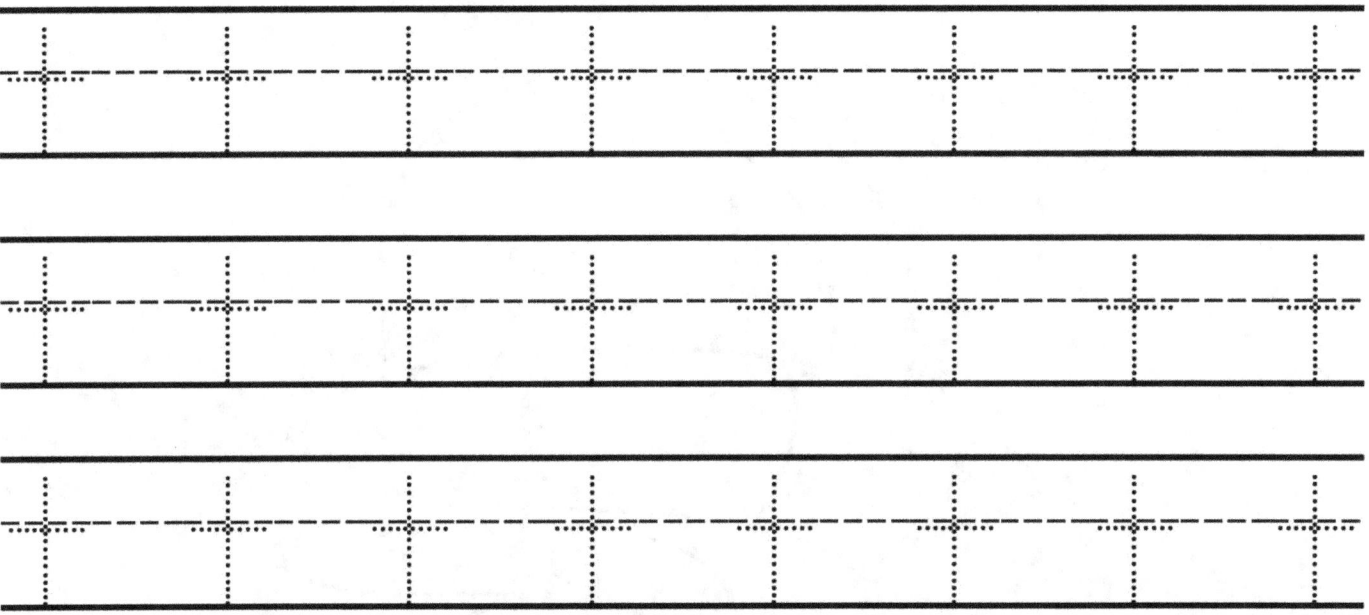

Now Write Letter t On Your Own

Uu   UFO

U _____

u _____

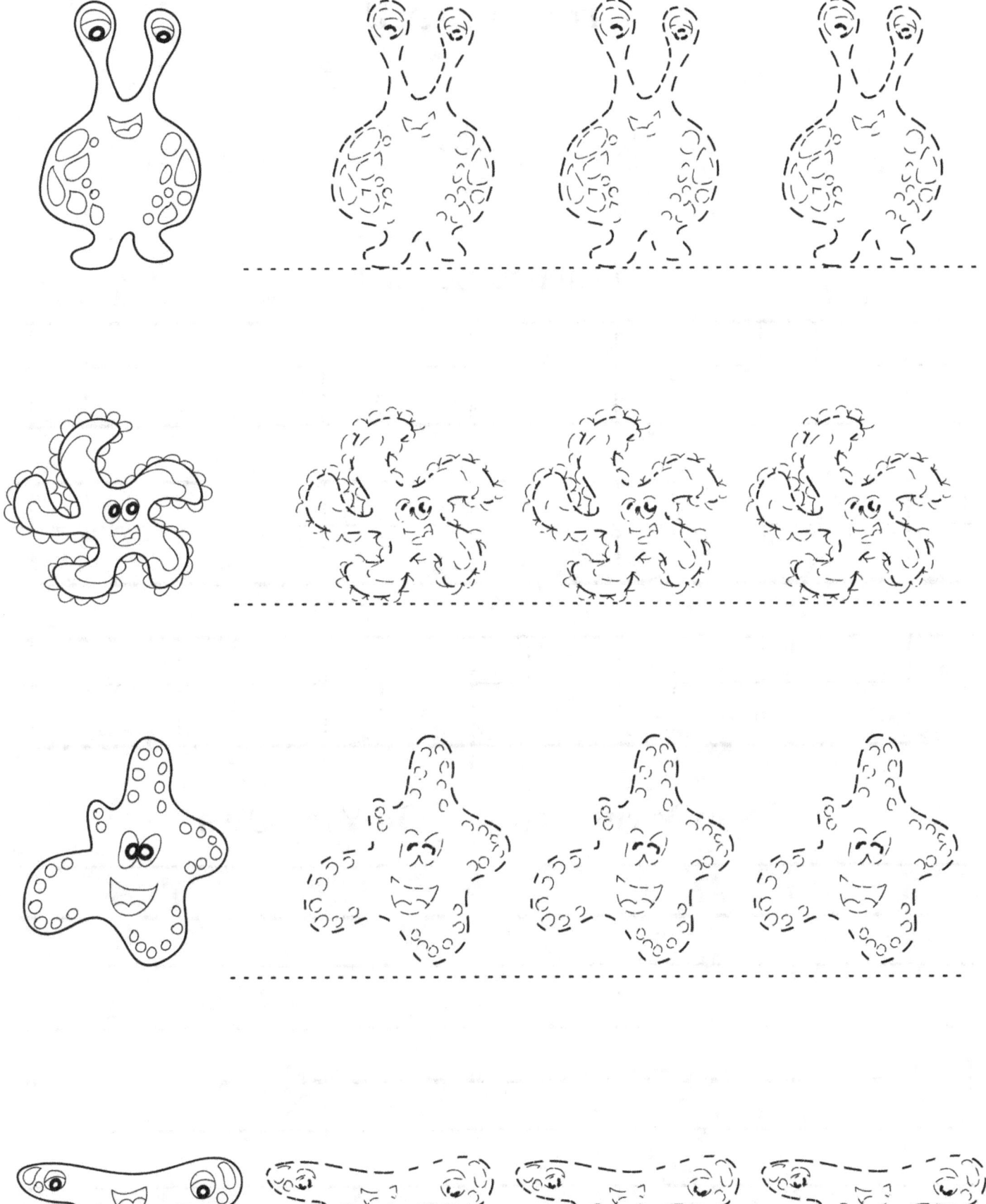

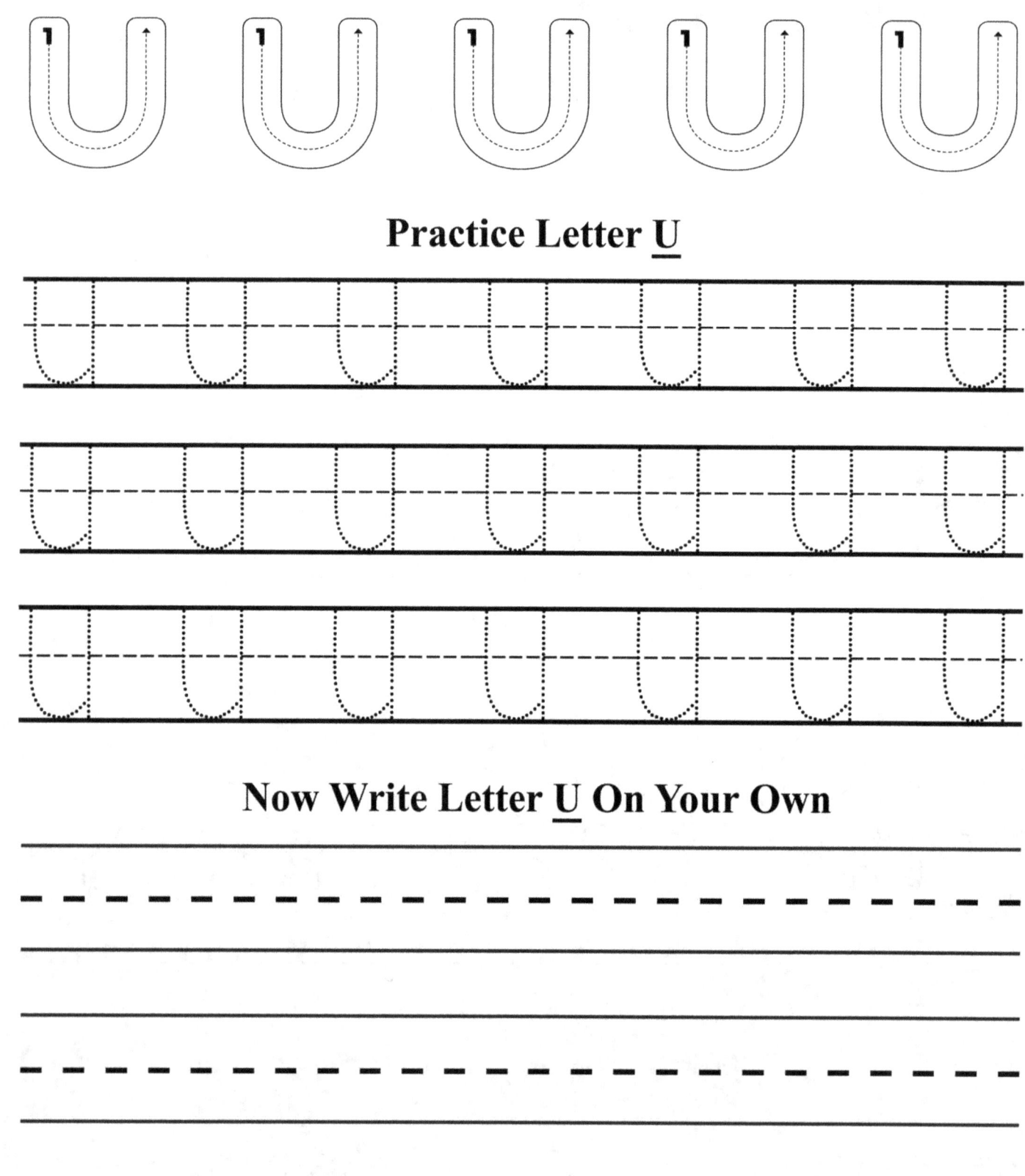

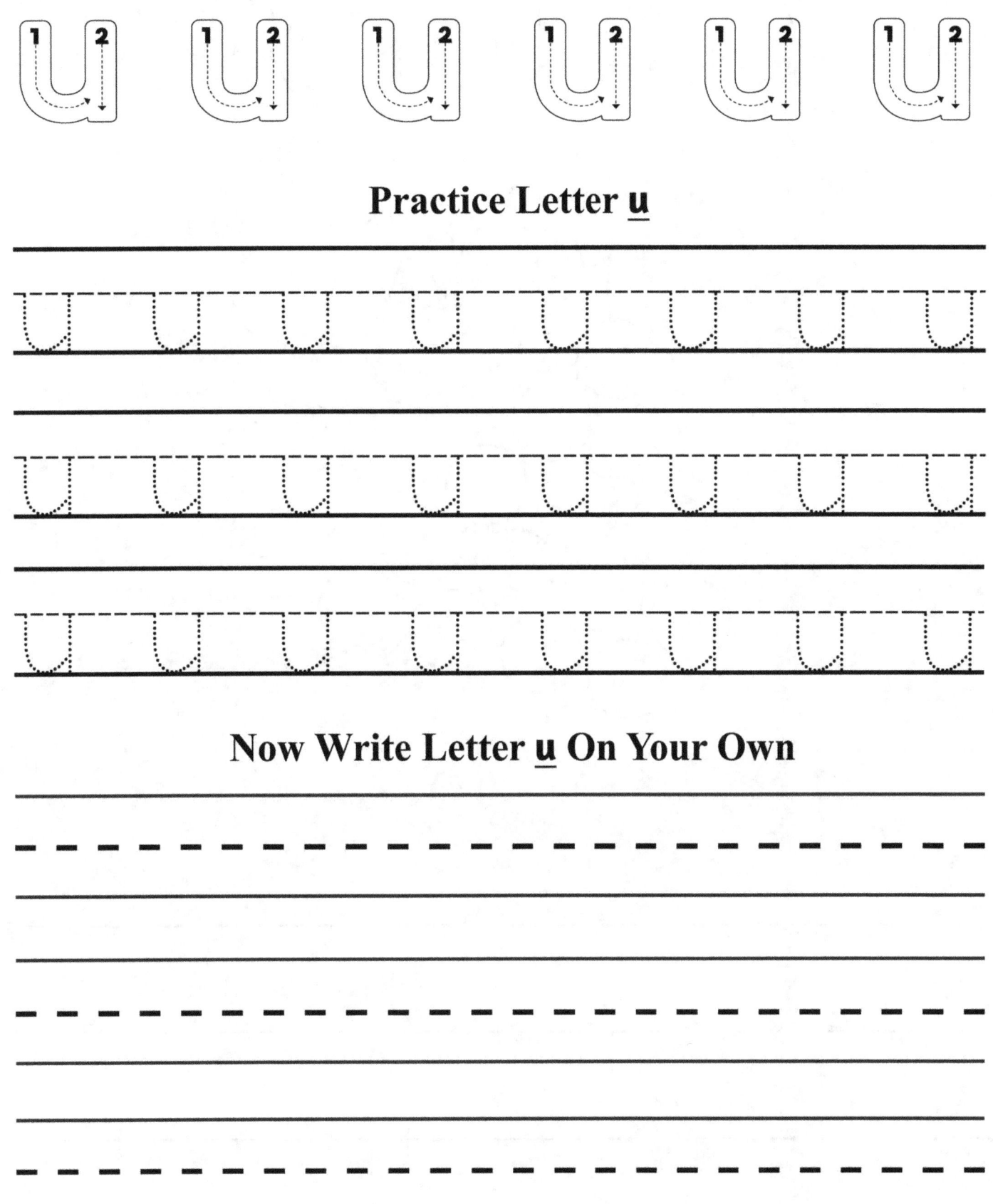

Vv Vineyard

V _____

v _____

Trace Letter V

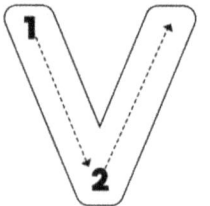 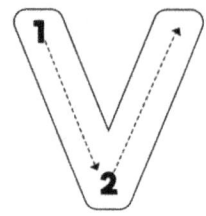 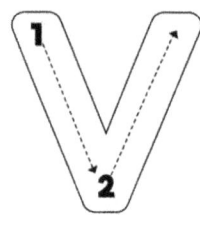 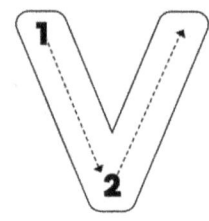 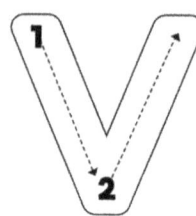

Practice Letter V

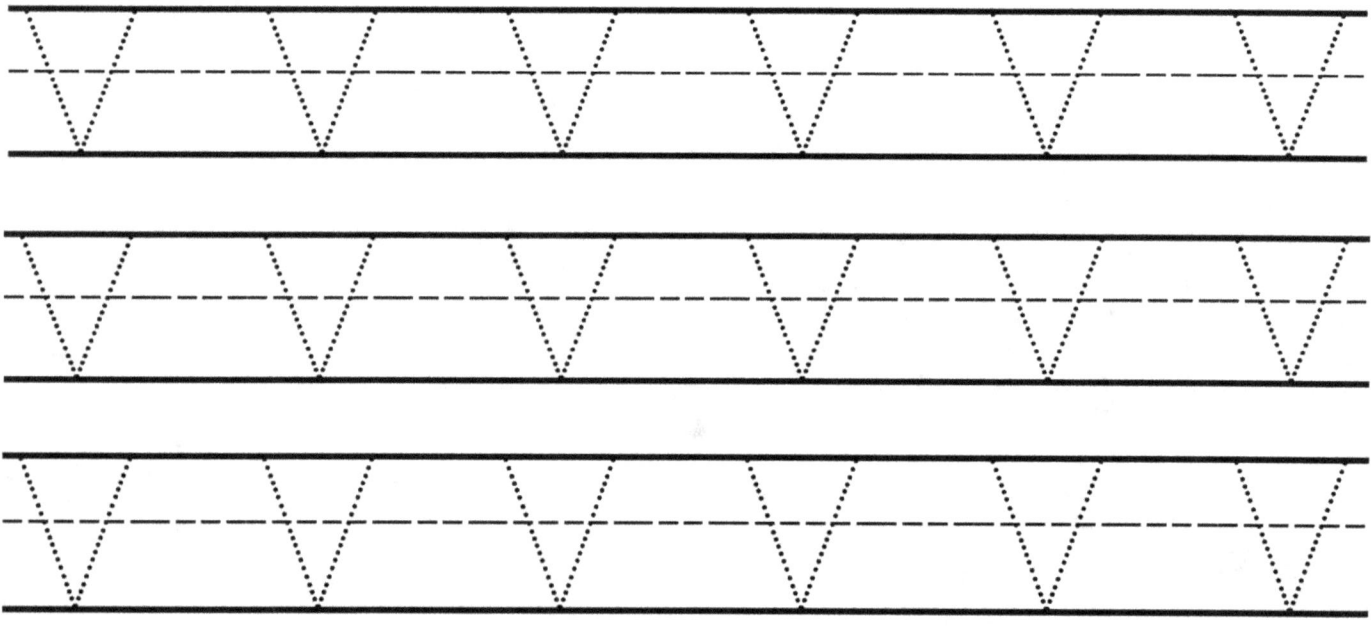

Now Write Letter V On Your Own

Trace Letter v

 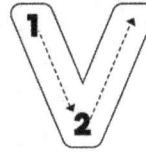 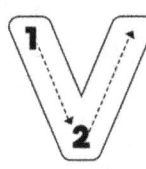 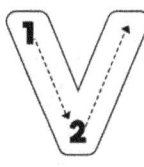 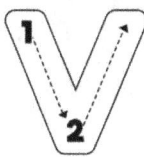 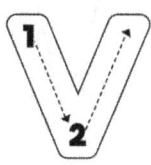

Practice Letter v

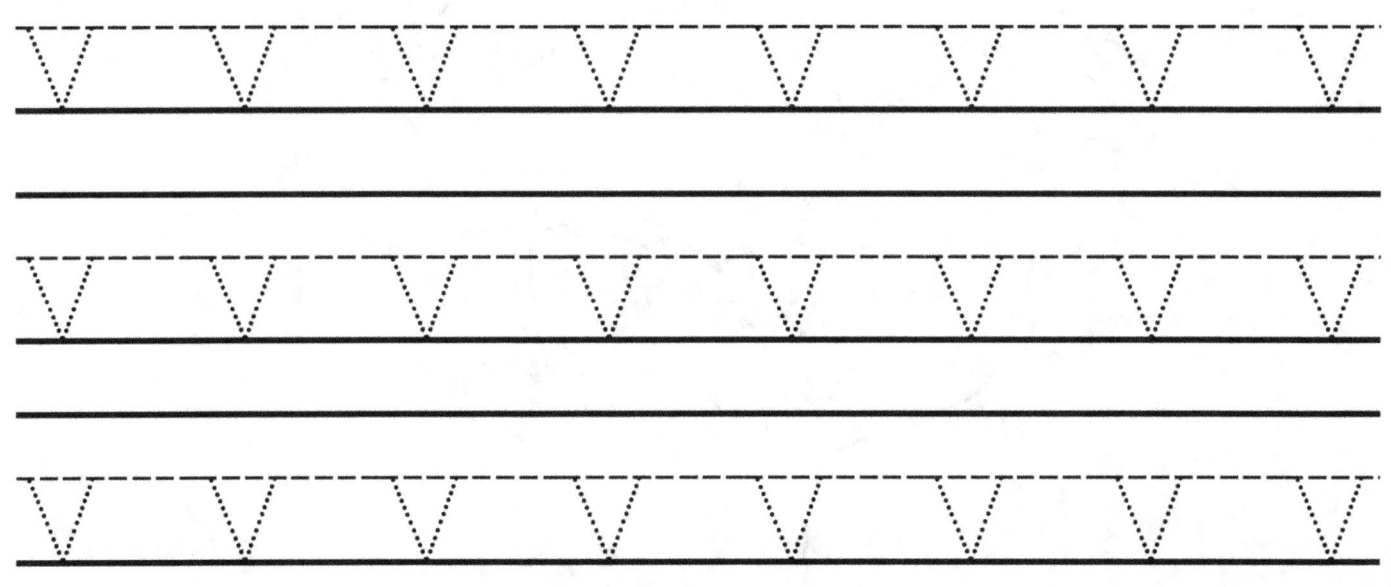

Now Write Letter v On Your Own

Ww   Wood

W _____

_____

w _____

_____

Trace Letter W

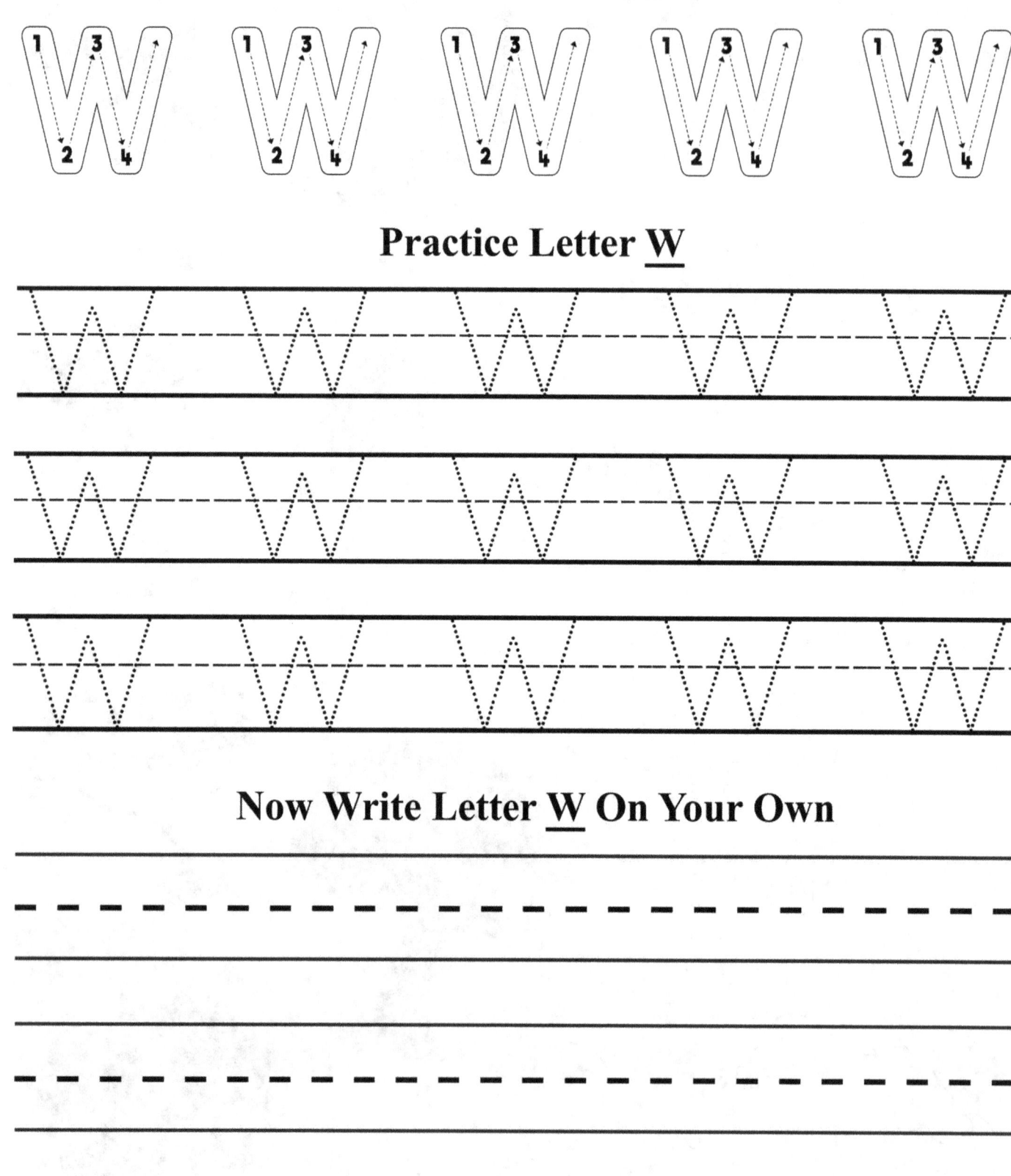

Practice Letter W

Now Write Letter W On Your Own

Trace Letter w

Practice Letter w

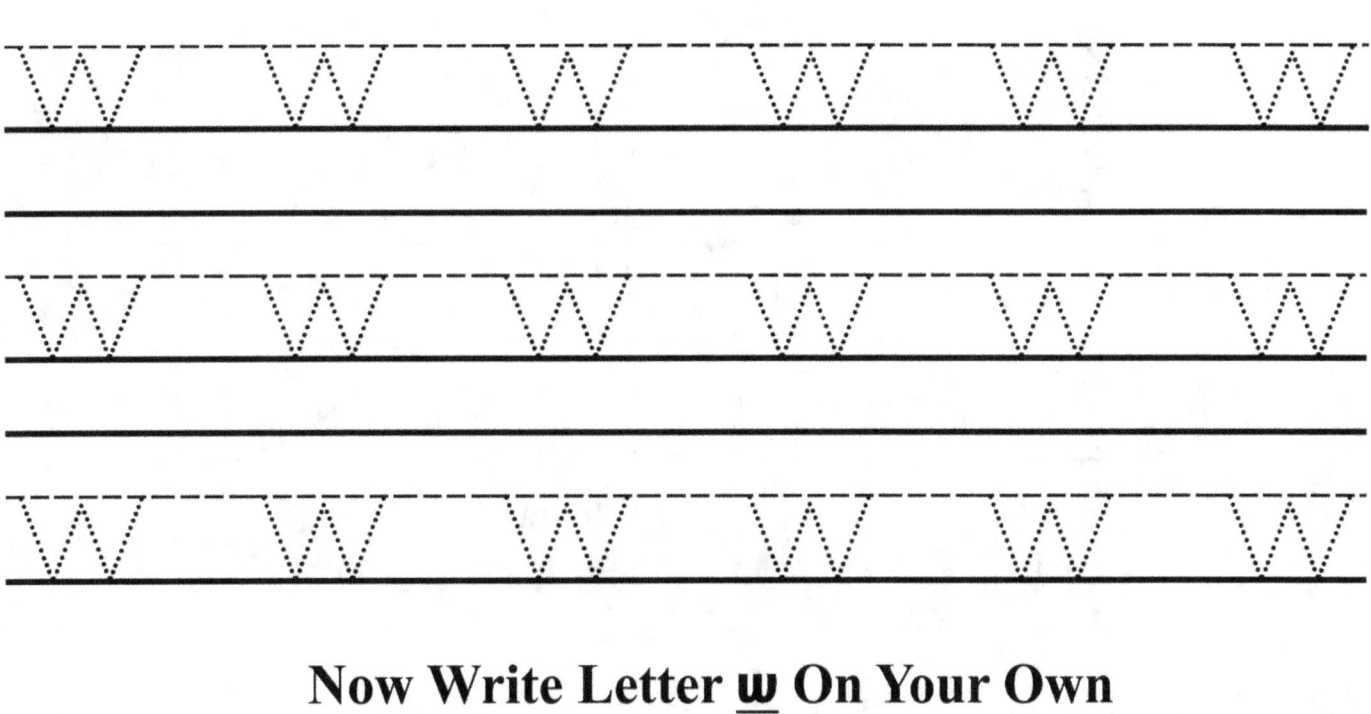

Now Write Letter w On Your Own

Xx X'mas

X _____

x _____

Trace Letter X

 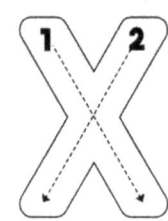   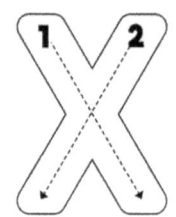 

Practice Letter X

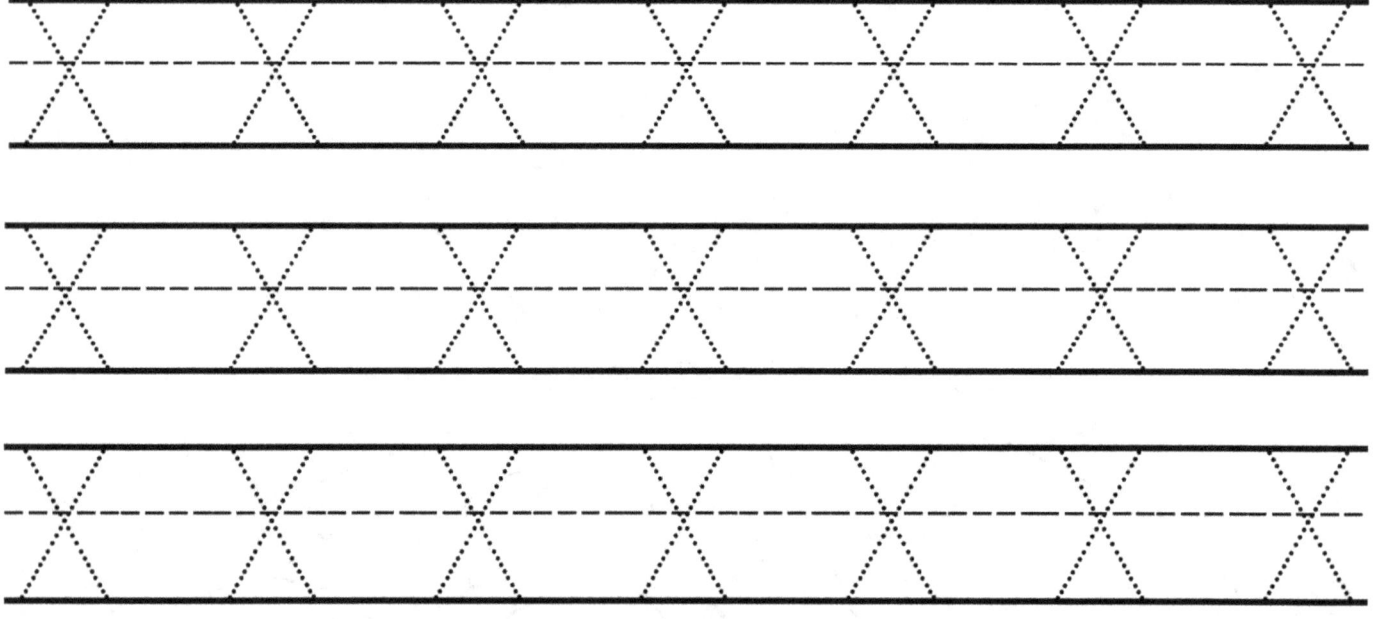

Now Write Letter X On Your Own

Trace Letter x

Practice Letter x

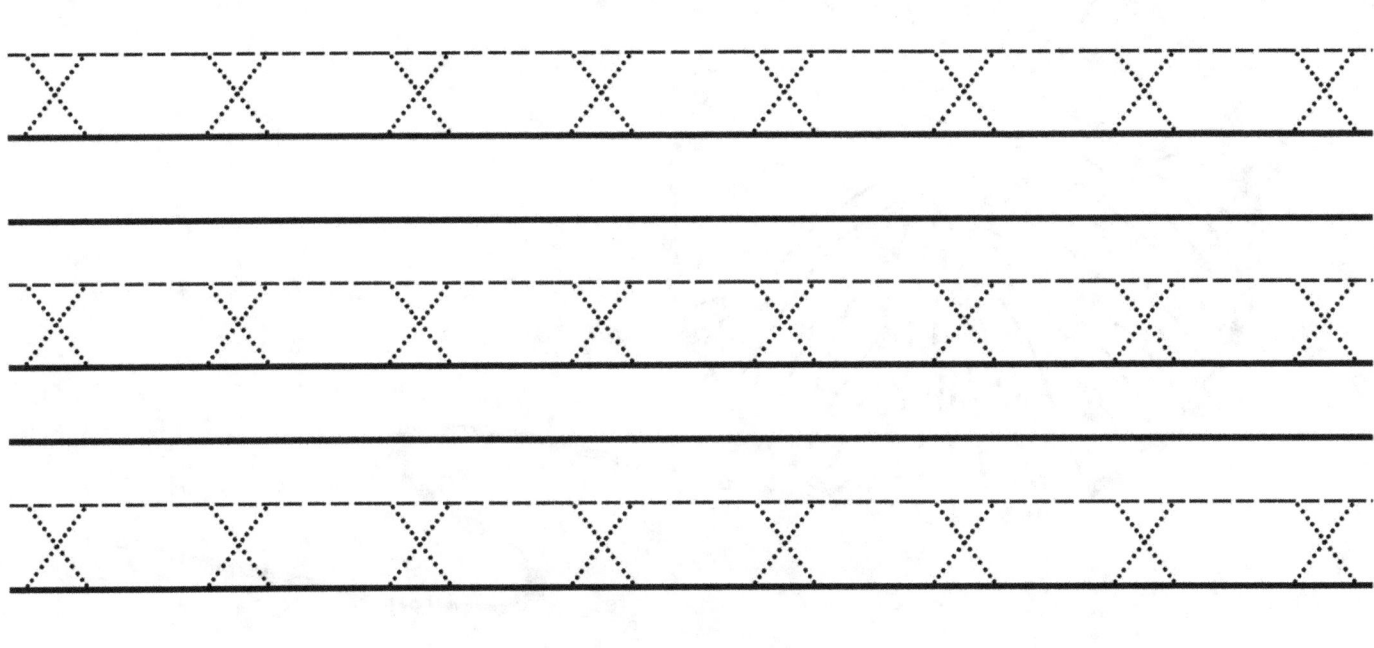

Now Write Letter x On Your Own

Yy Yarn

Y _____

y _____

Trace Letter Y

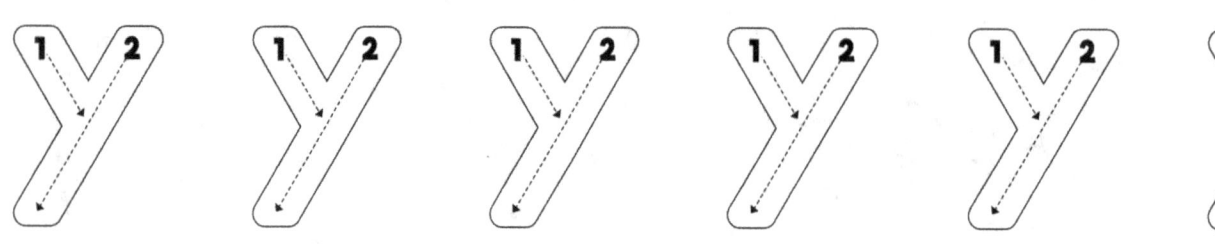

Practice Letter Y

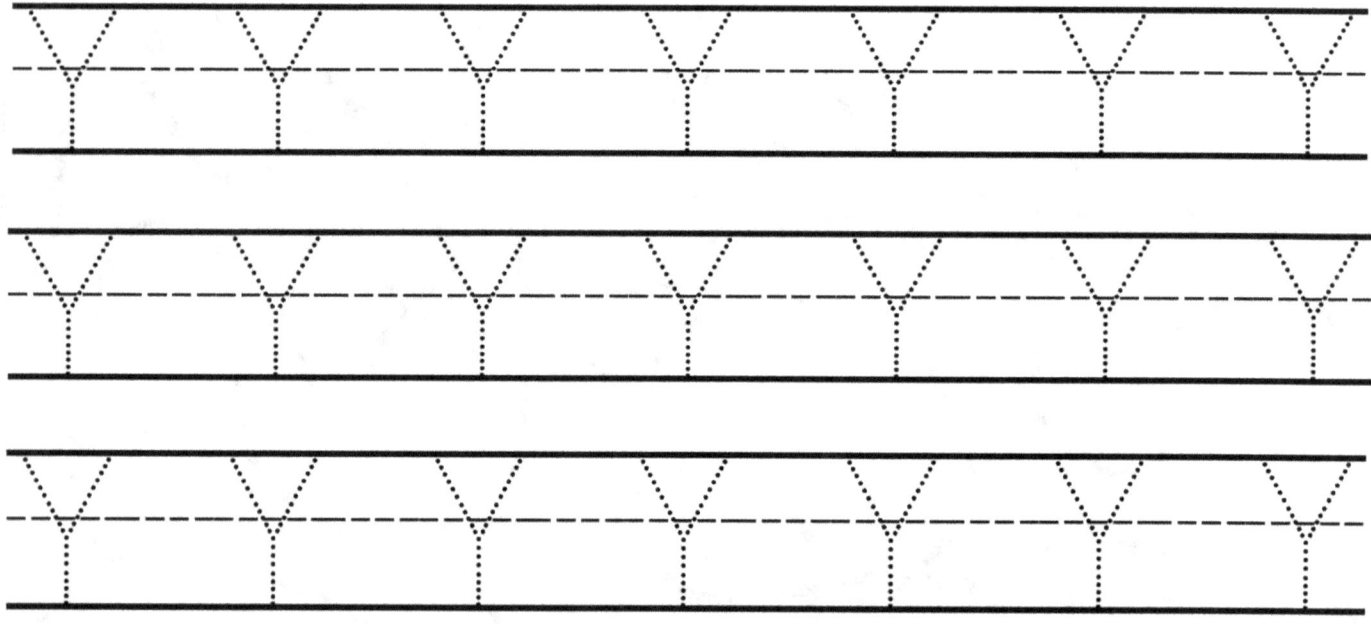

Now Write Letter Y On Your Own

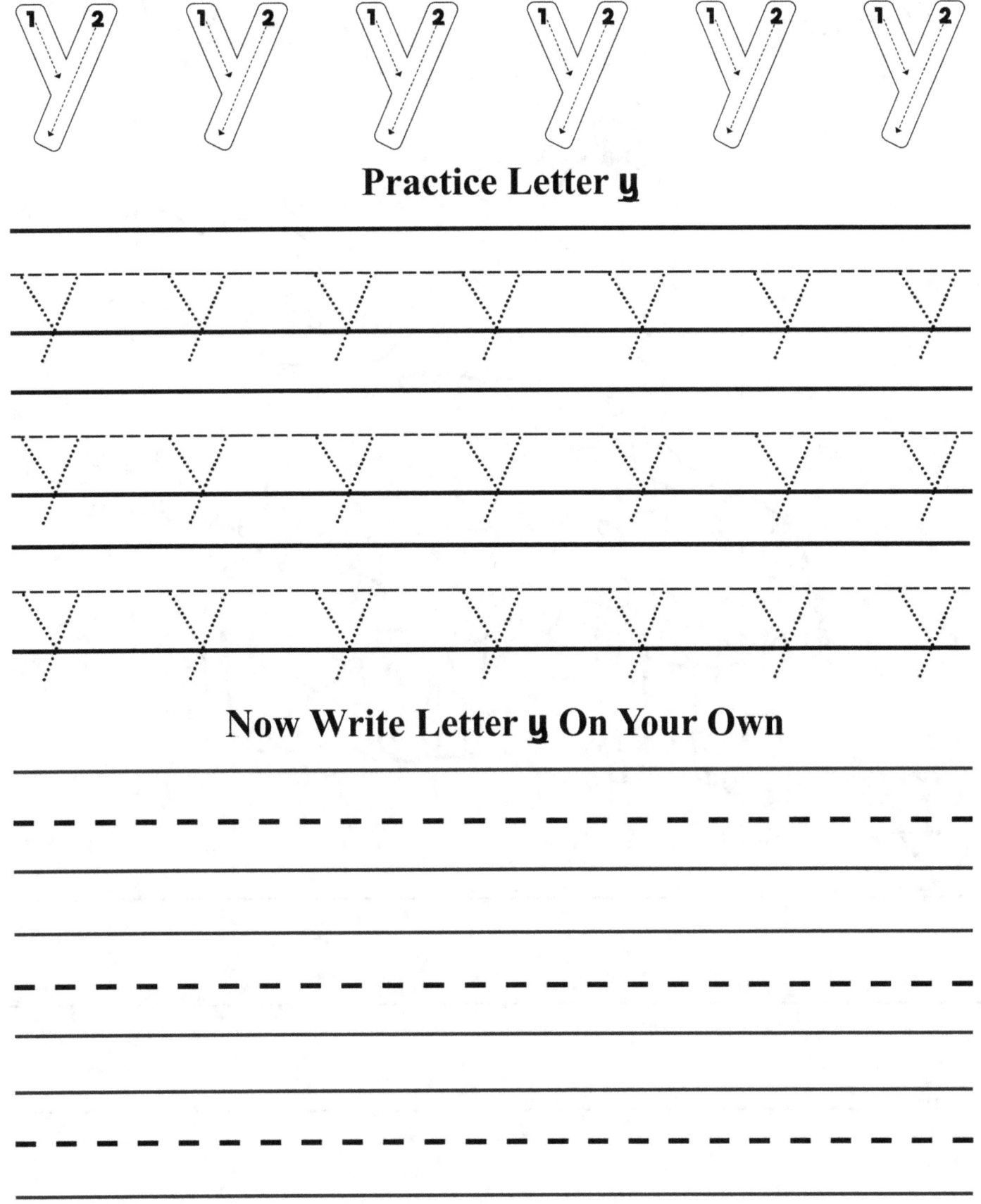

Zz Zoo

z _____

_____

z _____

_____

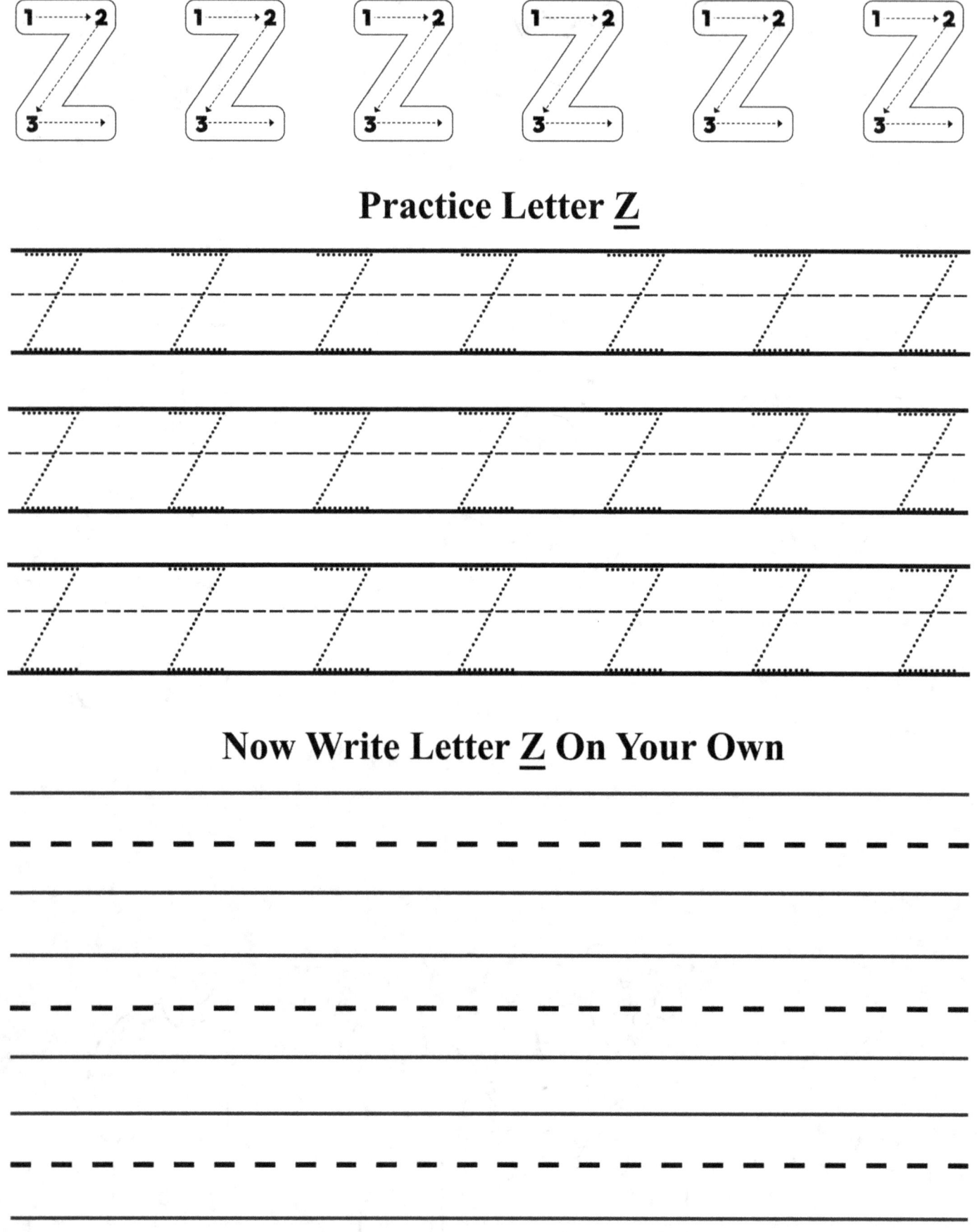

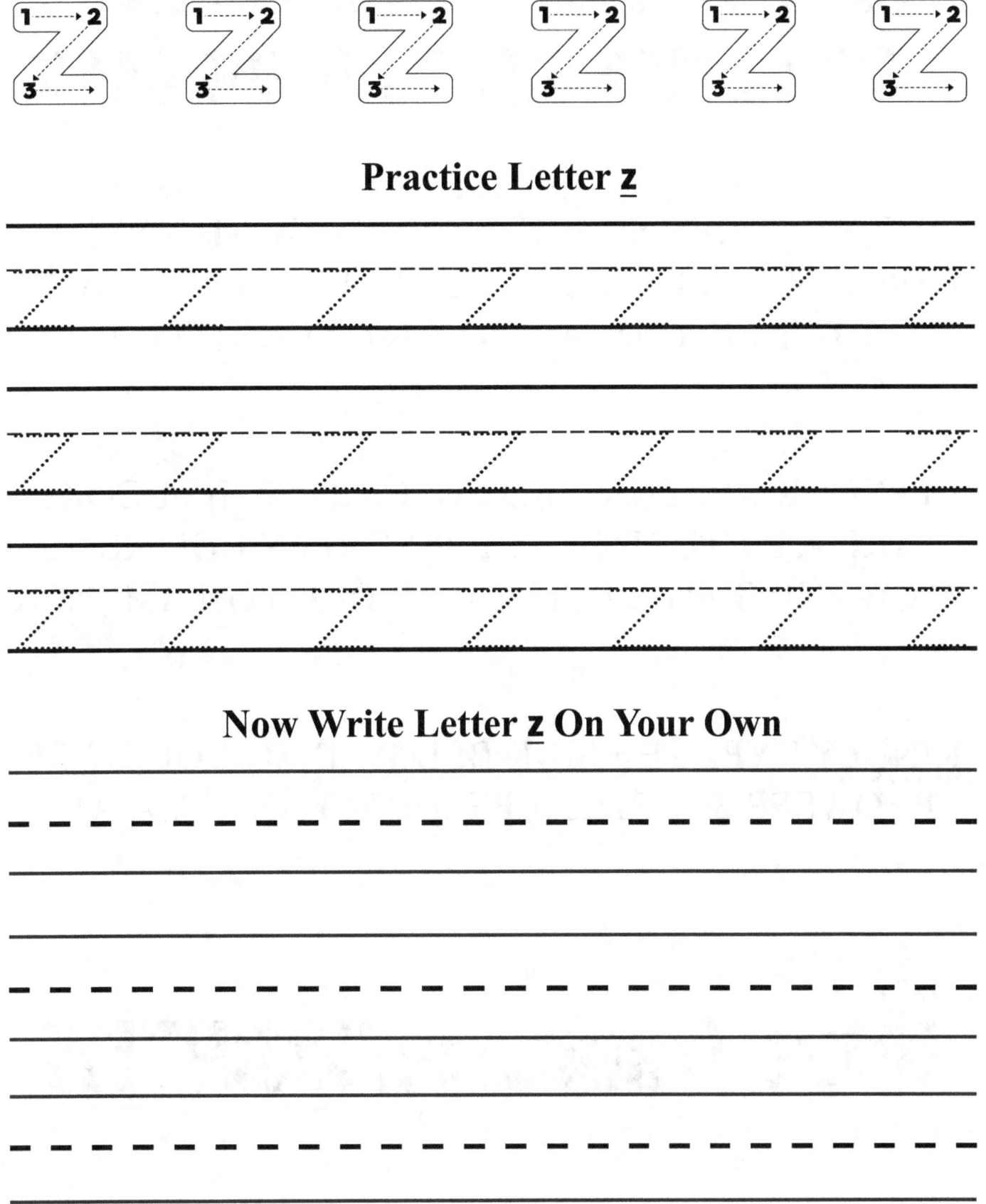

DID YOUR CHILD ENJOYED COLORING THIS A-Z ALPHABET COLORING BOOK

IF YES, THEN SHARE THE LOVE WITH YOUR FRIENDS AND FAMILIES OR GIFT THEM ONE AND LET THEIR KIDS ALSO CONTINUE THE FUN

IF YOUR KID ENJOYED COLORING THIS BOOK, TAKE A PICTURE OF THEIR LOVELY COLORING PAGE AND SHARE IT TO THE WORLD ON AMAZON

KINDLY TYPE THE LINK BELOW INTO YOUR WEB BROWSER & WRITE A FEEDBACK ON AMAZON

https://amzn.to/2xkNPIW

GET IN TOUCH WITH US

JOIN THE THRIVE COLORING BOOK ONLINE COMMUNITY

EMAIL: info@thrivecoloringbooks.com

WEBSITE: www.thrivecoloringbooks.com

FACEBOOK PAGE: @thrivecoloringbooks

PINTEREST: @thrivecoloringbooks

AMAZON: Amazon.com/author/thrivecreativekids

www.ingramcontent.com/pod-product-compliance
Lightning Source LLC
Chambersburg PA
CBHW060423220526
45465CB00008B/2994